BALDWIN

BALDWIN

ROY JENKINS

COLLINS
8 Grafton Street, London W1
1987

William Collins Sons & Co. Ltd
London · Glasgow · Sydney · Auckland ·
Toronto · Johannesburg

BRITISH LIBRARY CATALOGUING IN PUBLICATION DATA
Jenkins, Roy
Baldwin.
1. Baldwin, Stanley   2. Prime ministers
—Great Britain—Biography
I. Title
941.083'092'4   DA566.9.B15

ISBN 0 00 217586 X

First published in Great Britain by William Collins 1987
Copyright © Roy Jenkins 1987

Photoset in Linotron Meridien by
Rowland Phototypesetting Ltd
Bury St Edmunds, Suffolk
Made and Printed in Great Britain by
Robert Hartnoll (1985) Ltd, Bodmin, Cornwall

Contents

List of Illustrations

Preface

I wrote the first version of this biographical essay in the early seventies. It was conceived as a wing of a mansion which was to include portraits of American Presidents and of other British Prime Ministers. For reasons which I explained in the Preface to *Truman*, that rather grandiose plan I subsequently abandoned.

I have however considerably altered and somewhat lengthened *Baldwin*. Nonetheless it obviously remains an appraisal of his character and life rather than a detailed account of all their aspects. I have however kept to a chronological narrative, except for the substantial introduction, which attempts to set his career against the major issues of his age, whether or not he engaged with them. He was the dominant politician for fifteen of the twenty-one inter-war years. By any standards he must count, with Asquith, Attlee and Macmillan, as one of a quartet of major peacetime Prime Ministers (whose term of office is complete) of this century.

I have also added an appendix of potted biographies of many of the figures of the twenties and thirties who were associated with Baldwin. I thought of putting them as footnotes on the page, but decided that this would become oppressive. I suggest however that they are better read where the names are first flagged by a solid circle, rather than together at the end. I have not included Prime Ministers in the list of those of whom biographies are provided. I thought it otiose to explain who Churchill and Lloyd George were. As I needed a defensible frontier, this meant also excluding, perhaps less obviously, Balfour, Bonar Law, Neville Chamberlain and Eden.

I am grateful to Patricia Smallbone and Monica Harkin for typing the manuscript, to Diana Fortescue for checking it, and to my Collins editors, first Roger Schlesinger and then Helen Fraser and Alison Wade, for turning it into a book. I am also grateful to those who critically read the typescript, most of all perhaps to Lord Bonham-Carter. I received help with reminiscence from Lady Lorna Howard (Baldwin's second daughter), and with photographs from the 4th Earl Baldwin (Baldwin's grandson). Neither saw nor asked to see the typescript, and therefore gave their help 'blind', which is particularly kind. Of those I talked to about Baldwin, I think that the late Lord Boothby, in the last year of his life, gave me the most vivid impression, illuminating particularly the period of Baldwin's second and most important administration.

Introduction

It is forty years since Baldwin's death and fifty years since he last exercised power. During these decades his reputation has mostly been low, at best quiescent. It is difficult to imagine any of his successors in the leadership of the Conservative Party in the 'fifties, 'sixties, or 'seventies seeking to stir the faithful or to persuade the nation by evoking the great tradition of Baldwin to which they were heir.

Yet he has been by no means neglected by biographers, if not particularly well served either. At the time of his death in 1947 there had been three short studies, all of them by writers of some quality: A. G. Whyte's *Stanley Baldwin. A Biographical Character Study* (1928), Wickham Steed's *The Real Stanley Baldwin* (1930), and Arthur Bryant's commemorative *Stanley Baldwin*, written for his retirement in 1937.

The first posthumous and only authorized biography was G. M. Young's book of 1952, with the same simple title as Bryant's. It has been fairly described by Lord Blake as 'sketchy and inadequate'. It was also sufficiently unfriendly (see page 166 *infra*) to provoke published *ripostes*. The first was by D. C. Somervell, another Oxford historian and the elder brother of Baldwin's last Attorney-General (although this was little more than coincidental). It was of pamphlet length but lacked a true pamphleteer's style: there was too much gentlemanly rebuke and not enough polemical conviction. The second was a much more substantial *pièce justificative*: in 1955 A. W. Baldwin (Baldwin's second son, later the 3rd Earl) produced *My Father: the True Story*. This was a spirited and skilful filial defence, agreeably written and containing much (then) new information of interest. Obviously, however, it was in neither intention nor result objective biography.

Then, in 1960, John Raymond, a pyrotechnic literary critic, collected a series of essays of uneven quality and disparate content, under the title *The Baldwin Age*. Some of them had practically nothing to do with Baldwin, but Robert Blake justified his strictures of Young by showing what could be done with 12,000 words of straight biographical narrative. His essay remains not only the most succinct but also one of the most perceptive accounts of Baldwin's career.

Until the late 1960s however it remained the case that all the studies of Baldwin – A. W. Baldwin was on the margin of being the only exception – were notable more for their economy of scale than for the amplitude of the information they provided about their subject – perhaps as a sympathetic reaction to his own well-known economy of effort. (I am aware that in view of what I like to think of as the tautness of this book this comment may be regarded as an example of throwing stones out of glass houses.)

In 1969, any such paucity was superabundantly corrected. It was like a November opening of the heavens after a long summer of drought. Keith Middlemas and John Barnes assembled almost every possible fact about Baldwin and put them together in a volume (*Baldwin*) of 1100 pages and half a million words. The difficulty here is that, with so many facts present, trying to find one is like indulging in a lucky dip from a gigantic bran-tub. Like Churchill's pudding, this book lacks theme.

In 1973 it was followed by H. Montgomery Hyde's *Baldwin: the Unexpected Prime Minister*. Mr Montgomery Hyde was an Ulster Unionist MP in days when the representation of the province required less single-issue dedication than is the case today and is a professional biographer who has written on subjects from Oscar Wilde to Stalin. His book (250,000 words) was shorter than Middlemas and Barnes, but is nonetheless substantial. It is the best full-length study of Baldwin. It was followed in 1976 by another biographical essay, this time by Kenneth Young, formerly editor of the *Yorkshire Post*, who contributed *Baldwin* to a publishers' series, edited by A. J. P. Taylor, which embraced seven or eight Prime Ministers.

Since then there has been biographical silence. This is in a way surprising, for during these ten years Baldwin has begun to swim back into fashion. In part this is a function of growing nostalgia for his period of power, even though Baldwin himself was not a very obvious *art deco* product. Rather more, however, it is because Mrs Thatcher's brand of Conservative leadership has made him an object of contrasting interest in a way that Mr Macmillan's or Mr Heath's never did. When a new exponent of a different political style temporarily achieves notice – Mr Pym or Mr Hurd or Mr Biffen – it is now almost inevitably suggested that he might be a new Baldwin. That was emphatically not the case when Iain Macleod or Quintin Hogg illuminated the political sky. Nor even was R. A. Butler, who is now almost being amalgamated into a Baldwin/Butler tradition, much compared in his heyday with 'honest Stanley'. That was as well, for although Baldwin gave Butler the start of his thirty-three years of ministerial office and Butler cherished Baldwin's memory, it is difficult to think of two political careers of more contrasting shape, or two minds which worked more differently.

Baldwin's re-emergence into the arena of political comparison, whether or not the comparisons be accurate, does however make this a reasonable time for another look, written from a non-Conservative although not personally unsympathetic standpoint, at his neatly shaped yet most unusual career and his attractive but not profound character.

Baldwin had three major long-term issues with which to contend during his fifteen years as the dominant figure (for such he undoubtedly was) of British politics. These do not comprise either the sterling crisis and the formation of the National Government in 1931 or the Abdication in 1936. Both of these were important to Baldwin's life. The first determined how he spent his last seven years of activity, the second created the prestige with which he retired, although it could not make it last for long. But they were neither of them central, 'swell of the ocean' issues for the nation. The three in this category were: first, the thrust to power of the organized working class, expressing itself, alternately rather than complementarily, in industrial challenge and the rise to government of the Labour Party; second, the impact, felt for the first time, of Britain's relative industrial decline, which had begun as long previously as the 1890s, but which had been suppressed until our over-expanded and obsolescent basic industries ran into the export slump of the 1920s; and third, Mussolini's threat to a rather flimsy world order, which quickly became subsumed in Hitler's more massive threat to the independent existence of British (and French) democracy.

Brooding upon these issues certainly did not dominate Baldwin's life, although he left himself more time for thought than has any other Prime Minister since Balfour, and the general habit of his mind was ruminative rather than executive. But if they did not dominate the life of Baldwin they dominated the age of Baldwin, and his reputation in history must inevitably depend upon the view taken of his handling of them. In the early autumn of 1936 he was able to tell his Foreign Secretary, almost with the relieved exhilaration of a man who is freed of humdrum tasks by an exciting emergency, that he must not expect him to have time to spare for the Spanish Civil War and other dismal problems until 'the King's matter' was settled (page 148 *infra*). It was difficult to sell such an order of priorities to Anthony Eden at the time and it would be impossible to sustain it today. Baldwin's life must be described in terms of his own priorities, for they determined how he passed his time. But he must be judged in terms of the big issues of his epoch, independently of the extent to which he chose to engage with them.

He is strongest on the first issue, the handling of the thrust to power of organized labour. In his first year as leader of the

Conservative Party he had to roll with the punch of making way for the first Labour Government in British history – and one of the earliest in any bourgeois democracy. And in his third year he had to meet the unprecedented challenge of a full General Strike. The former was not in accordance with his immediate desires, for no Prime Minister could welcome giving up the office he had held for barely eight months in the wake of a severe setback at an ill-judged election. But it was in accordance with his longer term view of the desirable evolution of politics. He wanted a house-trained Labour Party to redress the balance of the party system which had been upset by the quarrels in the Liberal Party. No doubt he wanted the Labour Party to do it in a less self-confident and power-commanding way than either the Gladstonian or the Asquithian Liberal Party, but even more did he want them to do it in a way that blotted out the prospect of a centre party which could be a vehicle for the return to power of the evil genius of Lloyd George. Baldwin was as committed a two-party duopolist as Mrs Thatcher or Mr Kinnock.

From this point of view the very weak MacDonald Government of 1924 (with only 191 seats in the House of Commons) and the fairly weak MacDonald Government of 1929 (289 seats) served his purposes well. The rigid but unradical 'exclusivity' of the Labour Party, which meant that they would rather take their economic policy from J. P. Morgan and Company than from the Liberal Yellow Book, neatly matched Baldwin's 1920s view of how Britain should be governed.

There were therefore no great difficulties for him personally about MacDonald being summoned to Buckingham Palace in January 1924. What he had publicly anticipated nearly a year before had merely come to pass rather earlier than he expected or wanted. Nonetheless it must have been a considerable shock to many of those he represented – the conventional elements in a deeply class-conscious nation. The British Court and Government, while free of some of the rigidities which had recently been swept away from Vienna and St Petersburg, were still organized as the regal fount of the greatest imperial power the world had seen. Whitehall, the armed forces and the Palace had of course been recently used to seeing Lloyd George, with his *parvenu* classlessness, in the supreme political position, but it was nonetheless a substantial further step to see a Prime Minister who was not even a Privy Councillor because he had never held any office, and who moreover had been a pacifist in the war, leading a Government largely made up of 'working men' (to use that now archaic but then appropriate phrase) into positions, if not of great collective power, at least of high individual prestige. Nor probably was it made easier by the fact that he also led them, in the intervals of their being told how to behave in Cabinet by Lord Haldane and at tea by Mrs Sidney Webb, to struggle into frock coats and even levée dress.

That Government achieved little radical reform, let alone socialism, except for some sensible foreign and housing policy changes, and lasted a bare ten months. But the fact that it had come relatively smoothly into office, passed off calmly, although leaving a legacy of some bitterness about the methods of its electoral defeat at the end, and, few doubted, had set a precedent which would be repeated, owed a great deal to Baldwin. At the beginning he was in favour of the experiment not only because it fitted in with his view of the future of party politics, but also because it was the course which involved least casting around for new combinations in a Parliament without a majority, and therefore least threatened his position as leader of the defeated party. During its course he confronted it with little factious (or fractious) opposition. And when it was over he uttered the minimum of taunts about its shortcomings.

Against the 1929 MacDonald Government Baldwin was if anything even more restrained. This was partly because he was then so occupied with the twin challenges to his own leadership, the one about India, the other about tariff reform, that he had practically no time to spare for the Government. This lack of partisanship was however endemic with Baldwin, and was just as much a third cause as a result of his leadership troubles.

Baldwin out of office was a fish out of water, but he did not resent such turns of the political wheel nearly as much as do most politicians. He liked the longer holidays, and he lacked both the messianic conviction and the self-pity which might have made him feel cheated. Partly in consequence, weak MacDonald Labour Governments were subjected to much less bitter opposition than was the strong Attlee Government of 1945. This assisted the somewhat sickly infancy of Labour in government and meant that by 1930 quite a respectable attempt at a new two-party balance had been created.

Then, in 1931 (see pages 122–30 *infra*), Baldwin allowed himself to be a reluctant but nonetheless crucial party to an unnecessary upsetting of this delicate balance, to the creation of which he had devoted a substantial part of his efforts over the previous nine years. This came about through a mixture of indolence and too great a readiness to be persuaded against his own instinctive judgement by a contrary build-up of the forces of conventional wisdom. The result was the gross imbalance of British politics in the thirties, an uncomfortable four years of half-occluded power for himself, and a substantial offset to his previous well-earned reputation for influencing the broad lines of political development with wisdom and foresight.

The industrial thrust of labour he necessarily handled differently. He was a great exponent of emollience in industrial relations, both in his recollections of what life had been like when he worked in his family firm and as a principal weapon in his House of Commons armoury. But he had no desire, comparable with his approach to the 1920s Labour Party, to share power with Herbert Smith and A. J. Cook, the miners' leaders of the General Strike period. Nor, of course, did the Labour Party, not merely of MacDonald but of Henderson and Clynes too, have any desire that he should do so. The General Strike was as great an embarrassment to them as it was a challenge to Baldwin. They were almost as relieved as he was when he got it over in nine days.

Did he handle it well? On the whole, the answer is 'yes', provided a sharp distinction is drawn between the General Strike itself and the coal dispute, which was both the cause and the relict of the Strike, dragging on for another six miserable months after the collapse of the general challenge. Baldwin postponed the Strike for a year by a combination of subsidy and the Samuel inquiry, used the interval to make some sensible defensive preparations, faltered somewhat during the final phase of the pre-Strike negotiations, but probably not in a way that made any difference to the main sweep of events, was firm but calming during the Strike itself, and avoided the language of humiliation when he had won.

He did however allow the Trades Disputes Bill to become law a year later. The provisions of this Act do not today appear extreme in the context of current trade union legislation discussion, but they were bitterly resented at the time and for twenty years subsequently (until repealed in 1946), and were considered by Lord Blake (writing in 1960) to stem from an undesirable 'surrender to his own right wing'. This he attributes to 'the state of exhausted apathy' into which Baldwin typically fell after the main crisis was over. Whether or not this explains the Trades Disputes Act (similar legislation was nearly presented, without Baldwin's opposition, during the Strike itself), it was certainly a fact and made Baldwin (unlike his Chancellor of the Exchequer, Churchill) barren of resource during the long months while the coal dispute ground its way to a bitter and expensive end. The cost was a good 5 per cent of the national income, and dragons' teeth were sown deep in what was then, by a large margin, Britain's major industry.

Baldwin's remaining years of power did however see a great reduction in strikes, but also a growing involvement of the unions in consultation on a much wider range of issues than wages and the length of the working day. The first point was epitomized by Ernest Bevin reacting furiously to the formation of the National Government in 1931, not with the remotest contemplation of industrial action, but by deciding to offer himself as a Labour candidate (he chose Gateshead with little more concern than someone selecting a cigarette from a case, and was beaten by 13,000 in a seat which in 1929 had a Labour majority of 16,000). The second was exemplified by the Mond–Turner talks towards the end of Baldwin's second premiership and by the increasing tendency of the TUC during his third premiership to talk directly and robustly to the Government on international affairs without worrying much about the sometimes more equivocal attitude of the Labour Party.

Overall, therefore, it would be wrong to regard the Baldwin fifteen years as having disadvantaged the unions. He had resisted the General Strike, but so would have any other likely alternative Prime Minister of the period. He had not deliberately caused it, in spite of some equivocation in his negotiating behaviour during the forty-eight hours before its start.

He could however be accused of having inadvertently created the circumstances out of which it was spawned. This he did by allowing Churchill to take sterling back to the gold standard in April 1925, and at the old pre-1914 parity. Britain faced the world of the twenties with overexpanded, rather out-of-date basic industries geared to export markets which were no longer there. Some difficult adjustment would have been necessary in any event. To revalue the currency by approximately 10 per cent was to guarantee that the operation took place not merely without an anaesthetic but with the nerves specially sensitized.

Churchill hesitated over the foolish decision. He then accepted the determined advice of the official Treasury and the Bank of England. Baldwin appears to have given no consideration to this crucial decision of the administration over which he presided. This was the down-side of his devolved and relaxed methods. He sought to govern by mood creation rather than by decision. This meant that others were liable to take decisions which contradicted the mood he sought to create.

After his electorally unfortunate lurch towards protection in

1923, Baldwin did not seek to impose economic policy. Although his pre-Prime Ministerial experience of office (exiguous by most standards) was exclusively in economic departments – four years as Financial Secretary to the Treasury, nineteen months as President of the Board of Trade, seven months as Chancellor of the Exchequer – his practice in 10 Downing Street was to reserve his energies for the wider politics of the office and to leave the economics to his Chancellor. He gave as great a freedom to Churchill, whose approach was broad-brush, as to Neville Chamberlain, who was informed and meticulous. In the National Government it was MacDonald who a little mistily sought wider international solutions, as with the London Economic Conference of 1933, and Chamberlain who dealt not at all mistily with the nuts and bolts. Baldwin was the man of party power behind the facade of MacDonald's leadership and was Chamberlain's political chief. But it is difficult to trace much direct Baldwin influence on economic policy beyond a predisposition towards 'sound finance', provided dogma was avoided and the knots of public expenditure meanness were not pulled too tight.

Baldwin's reputation cannot be equally detached from the economic performance during his years of power. Until recently this was generally held to be a substantial count against him. A man who fought the general election of 1929, when unemployment was over 1 million, on a slogan as static as 'Safety first', and who then held power for over half of the 1930s years of distressed areas, basic industries without orders, and men without work, must surely have been guilty of a complacency verging upon discreditable negligence. The summing up of even such a right-wing commentator as Harold Wincott in the 1960 essays was that 'if in economic terms the Baldwin Age was a bad age to live through it was a good age to learn from' (and the lessons he thought had been learnt were the avoidance of deflation at home and of ill-ordered currency movements abroad).

More recent events enable a more favourable gloss to be

put on the performance of the Baldwin governments than in those bad old days when Macmillan was following Attlee, Churchill and Eden down the primrose path of full employment. In 1986 the Baldwin record looks a great deal better than it did in 1956 or 1966 or 1976. The 1.2 million unemployment figure which Baldwin handed over in 1929 had risen to 2.8 million by the end of the Labour Government in August 1931. Under the National Government it continued to rise, but more slowly, for another eighteen months, so that it almost touched 3 million in the first months of 1933. This peak represented a higher percentage (18.5 per cent) than the same figure would today, because of a smaller population and fewer women within it seeking to work. The geographical incidence of the unemployment was even more concentrated than today. Wales had an unemployment figure of 34 per cent, and Scotland of 26 per cent. Unemployment was also associated with a more abject level of absolute poverty than is the case today.

All that said, unemployment at these levels was a much more short-lived phenomenon in the 1930s than in the 1980s. Already by the time of Baldwin's last general election in 1935 it was below 2 million. By the time of his retirement in 1937 it was down to 1.5 million. The prospects for an unemployed man in 1931, particularly of course if he had youth and mobility, were much better than in 1981.

To some substantial extent the improvement of the thirties stemmed from rearmament, and indeed it required not merely the threat of war but more than a year of war itself to eliminate unemployment entirely in 1940/1. But as the next and main count against Baldwin is his dilatoriness in repairing the nation's defences, it would be ludicrous to dismiss his unemployment record on the ground that he had secured an improvement only by squandering money on rearmament. Nor would it be true. The house-building boom, which was substantially a response to low interest rates (2 per cent bank rate from June 1932 until August 1939), was at least as significant as rearmament to the recovery and began several years earlier.

No exegesis could make the 1930s into a period of full employment and British economic renaissance. But the comparative performance was not quite so bad as was commonly assumed in the long years of post-war labour shortage. It is also the case that while the basic industries went through a very bad time in the first half of the decade, their capacity was not permanently destroyed. Work on the *Queen Mary* at Clydebank, to take a famous example, was suspended for two and a half years for lack of Cunard funds (until it was restarted with a Government subsidy), but the shipyard was not closed down or dismantled. The steel works, the coal mines, the heavy engineering plants, even the textile mills, all survived and were available to be called back into full use in their original or other capacities when first rearmament and then the war sent demand soaring.

The other indicators of the period presented a mixed picture. Real wages (obviously only for those in work) rose steadily and significantly. The first glint of middle-class standards began to touch the helmets of manual workers in the more prosperous industries and the more favoured parts of the country. There was a widening of the gaps between the unemployed and the employed and between the old industrial areas and the new Britain of arterial roads, semi-detached gabled houses and factories which looked like exhibition pavilions. Britain's overseas accounts were more or less in balance, although heavily dependent on the revenue from the foreign investments of previous generations. Agriculture remained depressed, and we imported two thirds of our food. Inflation was not a problem, although the sharp price falls of 1929–31 (5 per cent a year) did not persist, and there was even some gentle (and beneficial) upward pressure from 1934.

Baldwin presided over a vastly unequal society and somewhat stagnant economy disfigured by pockets of appalling poverty (but so, it must be said, did Lloyd George and Asquith before him and MacDonald alongside him) and did so with some complacency. But his record on unemployment was incomparably better than Mrs Thatcher's, and he witnessed no such precipitate decline of Britain's relative wealth as occurred between 1958 and 1973.

So we come to the third issue and what became the major count against Baldwin: that he closed his eyes to the threat of Hitler, neglected his country's defences, and was only narrowly saved by the subsequent exertions of others from being responsible for the end of a thousand years of independent British history. This was the view which, when Chamberlain's death in late 1940 removed the protection for Baldwin of having a rival in obloquy, was well propagated by mostly left-wing journalists, ruined the latter part of Baldwin's retirement, appeared to be endorsed in Churchill's *The Gathering Storm*, and was inadequately refuted by G. M. Young.

Should such a refutation have been provided by a more friendly and less barren biographer? It could not have been done on the ground that Baldwin did not carry the full responsibility for defence policy. Apart from the residual responsibility which must always rest with someone who held his high position, defence was one of the subjects, together with the management of the House of Commons and India, with the supervision of which he was specifically charged and was supposed to occupy his time, even while MacDonald was still Prime Minister.

Nor could it be refuted on the ground that Baldwin was a resolute anti-appeaser and that, had he remained in office instead of handing over to Neville Chamberlain, the dictators would have been met with a stern front of British resistance. Baldwin would not have pursued appeasement with the self-righteous energy which Chamberlain devoted to it. He would not have excoriated its opponents in the way that Chamberlain did. More important, he would never have clambered three times into a small aeroplane, in September 1938, to fly twice to Bavaria and once to the Rhineland.

We would therefore have been spared both the pretence that Munich was an agreement for peace and not a surrender, and the attendant foolishness of waving a piece of paper and talking about 'peace with honour'. Baldwin's lethargy had indeed already brought him one bonus before he retired. In the summer of 1936, Tom Jones (see page 144 *infra*) had tried hard to persuade him to take a German holiday and see Hitler in the course of it. That was not Baldwin's idea of a holiday, even when he was feeling more vigorous than in that summer. Assisted by Eden's opposition, he wisely declined. The advantage of this immobility was that, unlike his old enemy Lloyd George, his old protégé Edward Halifax, and his successor Neville Chamberlain, he was never in danger of succumbing to Hitler's meretricious charm. The disadvantage was that it made it easier for him to avert his mind from foreign disagreeableness.

Baldwin's objection to Chamberlain's foreign policy, however, stemmed almost entirely from style and not from substance. This came out clearly in his ineffective House of Lords speech on the Munich Agreement. There is no reason to think that he would have been prepared to fight for Czechoslovakia in 1938 any more than he was prepared to fight to prevent Hitler moving into the demilitarized Rhineland in 1936 (for which cause, it must be said, hardly anyone wanted him to contemplate fighting).

The 'low case' for Munich, as opposed to the totally indefensible 'high case' which Chamberlain theatrically presented on his return, is that it was a necessary but inglorious delay: necessary because at that stage British forces lacked the strength to fight Germany, and the Dominions lacked the will to do so; inglorious because it involved the betrayal of Czechoslovakia. This 'low case' was well deployed in Iain Macleod's *Neville Chamberlain* (1961). In part it is damaging to Chamberlain, because it is wholly incompatible with the 'high case', which he did not hesitate to deploy, the claim that he was a prince of peace who had brought back a brilliant and honourable diplomatic settlement from Germany. In part, and perhaps the more important part, however, it is damaging to Baldwin. He was not responsible for the attitude of the Dominions in 1938, although it could be argued that had he talked more to their Prime Ministers about the 'dismal subjects' of Hitler and the Spanish Civil War, and a little less about the Abdication, they might not have required the extra year of shock before they were prepared to go to war in 1939. What he was much more clearly responsible for was the relative deterioration in British arms, so sharp that while the Germans could not have fought against the British (and French) at the time of the reoccupation of the Rhineland in early 1936, the British (and French) could not fight against the Germans in late 1938. If this was a valid excuse for temporizing at Munich, the blame must rest with Baldwin. The decisions (or non-decisions) which determined the level of British preparedness in September 1938 were taken prior to his resignation in late May 1937.

Baldwin cannot therefore be acquitted of the charge that, during the period when he was indisputably in general charge of defence policy, either as Lord President and the leader of the biggest party in the coalition or as Prime Minister, the most menacing regime in modern European history, easily eclipsing in this respect those of both Napoleon and the Kaiser, was allowed to move on to a track of military superiority. The defence that remains is that no alternative Prime Minister would have done any better. It is not by its nature a strong one. Politicians get the credit when things go well, even if accidentally, under their stewardship. It is not usual to challenge the war-winning records of Lloyd George or Churchill on the grounds that Lord Milner or Lord Woolton might have done the jobs quicker. By analogy, it is not therefore reasonable to exculpate Baldwin on the ground that on the firm evidence of their public statements a government under Attlee or Samuel (the Liberal leader) would have been still slower to rearm, and that an earlier Chamberlain premiership would certainly not have produced a greater national resistance to the dictators. He had the responsibility. They did not.

There was of course one other 'alternative' Prime Minister available throughout the thirties. That was Churchill. It was not a very realistic alternative, in the sense that hardly anyone considered it remotely likely. But as he was there, the most senior (in terms of offices held) of all living politicians except for Lloyd George, eager for power, and in Downing Street within three years of Baldwin's retirement, he cannot be wholly excluded from consideration. D. C. Somervell's defence of Baldwin did not attempt to do so. He set himself to argue that had Churchill become Prime Minister in 1933 it would not necessarily have made all that much difference, and would certainly not have automatically prevented 'the Unnecessary War', as Churchill chose subsequently to call it.

Parts of Somervell's argument are convincing, but the whole is not. An earlier Churchill Government might easily not have avoided war, might have faltered over Abyssinia and again over Spain, might not have successfully stiffened the French, might have bungled parts of the rearmament programme. But it is nonetheless impossible to believe that it would not have provided a different, more urgent, less comfortable note of leadership, which would have led to an earlier strengthening of our defences and resistance to Hitler.

At the very least the whole national tone would have been different. Baldwin always believed in letting policies flow from national moods and in helping to create such moods by the tone of his speeches. It is therefore reasonable substantially to judge his defence policy by the most memorable passages of his speeches on the subject. There are three which are pre-eminent. The first was on 10 November 1932, when he told the House of Commons, 'the bomber will always get through,' and added, 'the only defence is offence, which means that you have to kill more women and children more quickly than the enemy if you want to save yourselves.'[1] The message was perfectly sensible (a good deal more so than President Reagan's claims for SDI), yet intangibly defeatist. It became a recipe for hopelessness rather than for action.

The second (it was the third chronologically, but as its thought was retrospective it fits more naturally into second place) was his 'appalling frankness' speech, again to the House of Commons. Describing the mood at the East Fulham by-election in October 1933, he said: 'Supposing I had gone to the country and said that Germany was rearming and that we must rearm, does anyone think that this pacific democracy would have rallied to that cry at that moment. I can think of nothing that would have made the loss of the [general] election from my point of view more certain.'[2]

The third was in the run-up to the general election of 1935, when on 31 October he addressed the Peace Society. 'I give you my word', he said, 'that there will be no great armaments.' The phrase was well drafted to leave room for manoeuvre, but by no stretch of the imagination did it sound a clarion call for preparedness. It fitted in well with the other two speeches. The 'pacific democracy' was to be massaged and nudged, but not challenged. The nudging was in the right direction, but it was not heroic. It was a method of leadership for which a case can always be argued. But it is not the only method. Not only was it not Churchill's, it was not Gladstone's, or Lloyd George's or Gaitskell's. Arguably, however, it was Franklin Roosevelt's, so it cannot be dismissed as being only that of petty politicians or leaders who are below the level of events. It did not serve Britain well in the mid-thirties. But it is not different from the way in which at least forty of the forty-eight Prime Ministers since Walpole would have behaved. Baldwin, like Asquith, was unlucky in having to engage at the end of his career with major events to the handling of which his talents were ill-suited. This engagement cannot be held to enhance his reputation. It should not be allowed to destroy it.

CHAPTER ONE

A Quiet Beginning

Baldwin's political career is of a deceptive shape. At first sight it looks almost perfectly balanced, fitting into the inter-war decades like a bordered picture into a frame. He first joined a Cabinet in March 1921, two years and four months after the Armistice. His last day as Prime Minister was 28 May 1937, two years and three months before the start of the Second War. He assumed the highest office at fifty-five. He voluntarily relinquished it on the eve of seventy, the only man of this century to have been Prime Minister three times.* He died at eighty, after a full span of the retired leisure for which he had so frequently sighed, both publicly and privately.

Yet the appearance of perfect shape is almost wholly illusory. In fact his career lacked balance. The long years of his party leadership exist almost in limbo. They grew out of little. Ministerially his experience was minimal: four years in junior office, nineteen months as a notably silent President of the Board of Trade, seven difficult and chastening months as Chancellor, and then an effort-free but unexpected arrival in 10 Downing Street. A year before there had been at least six members of the Conservative Party better known than himself. Once there, he held on to power for a long time, easily in successive periods of government, with unusual difficulty in opposition. Luckily for him, his opposition years were few,

---

* For a second or third premiership to begin, there must be a return to office after a break. The life of an administration does not cease with a general election, and a premiership does not necessarily start with a new parliament.

only three of the fourteen spanned by his leadership. He prided himself, with high justification, on being a great House of Commons man, but it was only from the Treasury bench that he could lead with ease and pleasure. The quintessential House of Commons rôle of leader of the opposition he never mastered. He reserved his deadliness for dealing with opponents in his own party, and had little to spare for use against the MacDonald governments. But in office he exercised a full but lazy authority. Churchill said quite simply: 'He was the most formidable politician I have ever known in public life.'[1]

There was however a complete and unsatisfactory finality about the end of his premiership. There was no continuing momentum of influence. Not only was the curtain rung down but the opera house was dismantled. Few consulted him. Fewer still quoted him with approval. He had handled many issues with skill and public spirit and good feeling, but he had no publicly recognized parcel of achievement which he could open from time to time and contemplate with satisfaction. As Prime Minister he had mostly been popular and happy, although bearing heavily even the limited press of public work which his economy of effort prescribed. He resented principally the returns to London after his long holidays in France and cherished periods at his house in Worcestershire. In retirement these resentments were removed. But much worse ones took their place. He was lonely, sad, even a little bitter. The eclipse, partly by his own desire, partly because of the overturning of the world in which he had governed, was too abrupt. Within a few months of his resignation he was politically dead; and the repose lost its savour as soon as it was uninterrupted by forced returns to the grindstone.

Thus the two and a half years between his resignation and the outbreak of the Second World War brought Baldwin, the epitome of a man looking forward to retirement, disappointment and anticlimax rather than satisfactory afterglow. They were however years of pleasure compared with the five which were to follow, when, with his successor Neville

Chamberlain first out of 10, Downing Street and then dead in six months, Baldwin became a target of resentment for the perils to which the nation found itself exposed.

These were only a few of the paradoxes of Baldwin's life and character. Others found expression in his provenance and education. He was the most self-conscious countryman amongst British Prime Ministers of the past hundred years or more. The unchanging nature of English rural life was one of his more effective and frequently recurring oratorical themes. It reached its apogee in a 1924 speech to the Royal Society of St George. He spoke of:

> The sounds of England, the tinkle of the hammer on the anvil in the country smithy, the corncrake on a dewy morning, the sound of the scythe against the whetstone, and the sight of a plough team coming over the brow of a hill, the sight that has been seen in England since England was a land, and may be seen in England long after the Empire has perished and every works in England has ceased to function. For centuries, the one eternal sight of England.*

This, like many of his other speeches, was prose of a high evocative quality. Its prophecy was inaccurate in both the letter and the spirit. Now, little more than sixty years later, with the Empire admittedly gone and only too many 'works' closed down, but with little of eternity used up, the brow of every hill in England may be searched in vain for the sight of a plough team. And the destruction of traditional rural life probably proceeded more rapidly during his premierships than during any other span of fifteen years. When he began, Hardy's England was little touched. When he ended, it had been deeply invaded by suburbia and the motor car. The change was not his fault, although he was guilty of the self-deception or

---

* Annual dinner of the Society at the Hotel Cecil, 6 May, 1924. Reprinted in *On England* by Stanley Baldwin, first published in 1926, with seven subsequent impressions between then and 1937 when it appeared as an early Penguin.

hypocrisy of pretending that it was not taking place. In 1935 he was still talking of 'the ploughman "with his team on the world's rim ..."'. His romantic nostalgia was wholly genuine, although his dislike of change from the countryside of his boyhood was probably more acute than that of those whose origins and lives were more deeply rooted in it.

Stanley Baldwin was not an English country squire. In the first place, although he habitually used the words England and English rather than Great Britain and British, he was doubtfully English, both in blood and temperament. From his mother he inherited a strong Celtic streak, half Welsh and half Highland. She was the daughter of a Wesleyan minister who never earned more than £160 a year, but who brought up five daughters (as well as two sons), and saw one of the daughters married to Rudyard Kipling's father, another to Edward Burne-Jones, a third to another painter, Edward Poynter, later president of the Royal Academy, and a fourth to Alfred Baldwin.

Alfred Baldwin was born in 1841 and died in 1908. He was an ironmaster – of the third generation – and not a landowner. He was born prosperous and died rich, but he never owned more than a few acres around his house. At first he lived in the town of Bewdley and then at Wilden, a moderate-sized semi-country house of the 1840s, but within sight and sound of the forge which was the old centre of the family business. He largely reshaped this family business, rescuing it from near bankruptcy in the 1860s, extending it into tinplate in Monmouthshire, carrying through several amalgamations, and turning it into a public company in 1902. He was also chairman of the Great Western Railway and Member of Parliament for the Bewdley division of Worcestershire from 1892 until his death. Yet he was far from being a conventional man of business. He abandoned Methodism early in life and became an extreme High Churchman. He was a scholar of neurotic temperament.

Stanley Baldwin was born in the house at Bewdley on 3 August 1867, within a year of the marriage of his parents. He was the only child. The house of his childhood was Wilden, where his mother gave him a literary upbringing. When he married he rented a rambling red-brick Georgian house two miles away and bicycled to work at the forge most days. After ten years he rented and moved to Astley Hall, near Stourport, a larger and older stone house with Dutch gables and a wide, soft view across the broken Worcestershire countryside. Later he bought this house, built a new wing, greatly improved the garden, and extended the estate from twenty to one hundred acres, mostly farmed by tenants. In the years between his father's death and the outbreak of the First War, this became quite a grand establishment. There were ten gardeners and about as many indoor servants. At that time he also maintained a large London house, at first in South Kensington, later in Eaton Square.

Astley he retained until the end of his life, despite mounting worry about the expense, and spent nearly the whole of his retirement there. During his ministerial years, however, he had used it relatively little – ten days at Christmas, a week in early August, and perhaps a couple of other visits during the year. Apart from the ties of London, he liked and used Chequers a lot, and had established the almost unfailing rhythm of a long late summer holiday at Aix-les-Bains in the French Alps. But his feeling for the triangle bounded by the Black Country, the Cotswolds and the Welsh hills was intense. He loved wide landscape and changing light, and it is very good country for that. 'It looked stormy but I risked it,' he wrote of a 1931 Boxing Day expedition with his younger son,

and we drove through Cleobury Mortimer on to the Clees. I never saw the views so wonderful. There was dark cloud to within a couple of yards of the southern horizon, below which a perfect golden background, and there was silhouetted every hill from Clent to the

Sugar Loaf by Abergavenny and the Black Mountains.
We drove down the Angel Bank skirting Ludlow, and
then as we turned into Corvedale the sun came out and
it cleared. . . . We drove home round the Brown
Clee. . . .[2]

The next day he motored to four miles south of Hereford to
lunch with an old cousin, and the day after that he attended
two funerals, both of 'old Worcestershire friends who died on
Christmas Day'. His agricultural knowledge was very limited.
He could not have milked a cow, and he poked pigs much more
often in cartoons than in the farmyard. But he was a genuine
West Worcestershire man, and the City of Worcester with its
tall cathedral tower, its county cricket ground beside the steep-
banked Severn, and its chocolate and cream Great Western
trains arriving at Shrub Hill Station from Paddington,* was the
centre of some substantial part of his life.

Baldwin was not educated in Worcestershire. He was the
first member of his family to receive a conventional English
upper-class education. His father had been to the Wesleyan
Collegiate Institution at Taunton until the age of sixteen, when
he had left and gone into the business. But Stanley Baldwin
was sent to Hawtrey's, near Slough, which was almost exclusively an Eton preparatory school, although there followed a
not wholly explained change of plan and he went to Harrow
in 1881. He started successfully there, as he had done at
Hawtrey's, winning academic prizes and achieving a fair success at games. Then at the end of his third year it all went
wrong. He was caught writing pornography and – worse still –
sending it to his cousin at Eton. Dr Montagu Butler, a notable
headmaster, who was also his housemaster, treated the matter

---

* Baldwin was always fond of railways, travelled by them whenever he could, was
an amateur of their timetables, and enjoyed his directorship of the GWR. He was also
good at getting around London by bus or tube. But he could never drive a motor car (he
liked to claim that the internal combustion engine was responsible for more human
misery than any other invention) and he never entered an aeroplane. In being unable
to drive he was no different from at least three of his successors, but he was the last
Prime Minister who never flew.

with a ridiculous portentousness. Alfred Baldwin was sent for. There was a flogging and the incident died down. But so did Stanley Baldwin's enthusiasm for Harrow. He became lazy and somewhat withdrawn. He left a year earlier than he need have done.

In later life there was some ambiguity about his attitude to the school. He was naturally nostalgic, even sentimental, and a respecter of established institutions with which he had been connected. He therefore never spoke ill of Harrow; and on one occasion he announced in a speech there that when he was first called upon to form a government he was determined to have the unprecedented number of six Harrovians in his Cabinet. But this was almost certainly an *ex post* joke, unless it was the only explanation he could offer for the remarkably un-distinguished collection of ministers who governed with him in 1923, most of whom he had in any event inherited from Bonar Law. There is no evidence that memories of the school ever played much part in his life, or that he particularly enjoyed visiting it. He sent his own two sons to Eton, with unfortunate results in one case.*

Nor was Baldwin in any way a notable Harrow figure. He was rather anonymous amongst his contemporaries, and the flavour of this anonymity is well captured by an anecdote, possibly apocryphal like most anecdotes, from much later in his life. During his second premiership he noticed during a train journey that another occupant of the compartment was look-ing at him with some puzzlement. After a time this gentleman leant forward and tapped Baldwin on the knee. 'You are Baldwin, aren't you?' he said. 'You were at Harrow in '84.' Baldwin nodded assent to both propositions. His former school-fellow appeared satisfied. But after a few more minutes

---

* This pattern of disloyalty has been curiously prevalent amongst Harrow's notably distinguished quartet of Prime Ministers of the past 150 years. Peel, Palmerston, Baldwin and Churchill were Harrovians. Churchill joined Baldwin in sending his own son to Eton. Peel deserted Harrow for Eton for his two youngest sons. Palmerston, who had no son, neither sustained nor contradicted the pattern.

he again became puzzled and tapped once more. 'Tell me,' he said, 'what are you doing now?'*

Baldwin carried both the anonymity and idleness of his last Harrow years with him to Trinity College, Cambridge. Also, by singular misfortune, he was followed by Dr Montagu Butler, who was translated to the Mastership of Trinity at the beginning of his second term. Whether or not because of the oppressive presence of the new Master, Baldwin, as he later saw things, largely wasted his time at Cambridge. He read history and achieved a steady deterioration in each year's performance. He got a First at the end of his first year, a Second at the end of his second, and a Third at the end of his third. But more surprising than his lack of academic prowess was his failure to make any other sort of impact. He made few friends; he joined few clubs or societies, and after being elected to the college debating society was asked to resign because he never spoke; he did not even spend much money. He was interested in the Trinity Mission in Camberwell, and at one stage his thoughts turned towards being ordained. But then they turned away again. He did however enjoy the physical beauty of Cambridge, and retained a strong affection for the place on this ground at least. He was delighted by the somewhat undeserved honour of the Chancellorship of the University, which was bestowed upon him in 1930, and which he retained to the end of his life.

He came down from Cambridge in 1888, and without either great enthusiasm or great reluctance went into the family business. For twenty years he served as second-in-command to his father. He had no desire to take over the first place. He worked with reasonable diligence, getting to Wilden by eight o'clock most mornings, and also travelling a good deal – to South Wales, to Birmingham, to London and even on one occasion to the United States – on the firm's affairs. He took

* The story is at least *ben trovato* in having Baldwin as Prime Minister travelling by train alone, which Asquith and Gladstone had done before him, but which no post-war occupant of the office, except perhaps for Attlee, would have thought of doing.

long holidays, habitually spending a winter month in Switzerland and a summer month or more in France or Italy. Despite the *persona* which he subsequently cultivated, he was not an insular Englishman. He could read French easily, and could manage some German. He knew pre-1914 Europe very well.

His energies were never enormous, but limited though they were, he used a large part of them outside the business. He accepted the semi-political duties of a man of substance in his county. He never had much enthusiasm for making money. He distrusted those who were too rapidly successful. He once shocked Bonar Law, who took a rather more respectful view of money matters, by saying that 'a man who made a million quick ought to be not in the Lords but in gaol'.[3] He liked a steady business, moving up rather than down, operating in not too competitive a climate, and able as a result to maintain a paternal relationship with the workpeople. This was almost exactly how Baldwins Ltd operated in the nineties.

In 1892, at the age of twenty-five, Baldwin married Lucy Ridsdale. He had met her while staying with his Burne-Jones cousins at Rottingdean, a Sussex coastal village which had not then become a suburb of Brighton. She was the daughter of a scientist who was at one time Deputy Master of the Mint. During the years of Baldwin's premierships she appeared a slightly ridiculous figure to the sophisticated young. This was due partly to her hats and partly to her remarkable prowess as a lady cricketer. Neither of these were fundamental criticisms. She was on the whole a very satisfactory wife. She did not share Baldwin's intellectual or aesthetic tastes, and she did not accompany him on the long walks which were a staple part of his recreation in Worcestershire or at Aix. But she provided him with loyalty, sensible advice and a closely shared experience of life for over fifty years. And she allowed others, notably Mrs Davidson (later Lady Davidson, MP), to take the walks.

The Baldwins had six children, two sons and four daughters, born between 1895 and 1904. The eldest son, who lived out his life as a bachelor of somewhat eccentric habits, became deeply

estranged from his parents as a young man. He joined the
Labour Party, and denounced Baldwin personally as well as
politically at the 1923 election. The personal break, although
not the political one, was later happily repaired. He was once
acting vice-consul in Boulogne, served in the Armeno-
Turkish war of 1920, was several times a Member of
Parliament, and ended his public career as Governor and
Commander-in-Chief of the Leeward Islands. He died relatively young in 1958. The second son, Windham or 'Bloggs'
Baldwin, the father of the present earl, lived a calmer life
enlivened by some association with the fashionable literary
world, and died in 1976. Three of the daughters married, all
respectably, none 'brilliantly'. One (Lady Lorna Howard) is
still alive. The fourth (Lady Betty Baldwin) spent some time in
a nunnery and wrote a mildly sensational book about her
experiences.

During his twenty years of more or less full-time business
Stanley Baldwin became a Justice of the Peace, the chairman of
a board of school managers and a member of the Worcestershire County Council. He made a few political speeches, mainly
in his father's constituency. In 1904, he became candidate for
the neighbouring borough of Kidderminster. It was a Con-
servative-held seat, and the assumption was that the next
election would result in two Baldwins sitting for Worcestershire. This did not happen. The 1906 election produced a
Liberal landslide, although it was much less strong in the West
Midlands than in most other parts of the country. Alfred
Baldwin held Bewdley, but Stanley was defeated at Kidderminster. He had not much enjoyed the campaign, and whether
because of this or of the result, he had to go immediately on a
two-day walk from Kingham to Oxford to purge himself of his
'humours'.

Neither the campaign nor the result purged him or his family
of a settled if unenthusiastic feeling that he ought to go into the
House of Commons. The member for Worcester City was on
this occasion one of the dozen or so gentlemen who, after most

late nineteenth- and early twentieth-century general elections, as a sort of ritual but somewhat haphazard sacrifice to
virtue made by an easy-going society, were unseated on
petition for allegedly corrupt electoral practices. Joseph
Chamberlain, who had held Birmingham and much of the
West Midlands firm for Unionism and Tariff Reform, suggested
that Baldwin should step into the seat. The Baldwin family
were strong for protection, which commended them to
Chamberlain. But it was not enough to commend Stanley to
the City of Worcester Conservative and Unionist Association.
They preferred Edward Goulding,* whom Baldwin described
as 'an Irishman, whom I then thought and think still, to be
vastly my inferior. So I was turned down in my own county
town in favour of a stranger . . .'⁴ It was one of the few
occasions in his life when he *tried* and failed. For some years to
come, his parliamentary prospects seemed blocked. It did not
occur to him to look for a seat outside Worcestershire, and even
if it had there was little reason why he should have secured
one.

Then, in February 1908, his father died suddenly. Two days
after the funeral Stanley Baldwin was selected as candidate for
Bewdley. Before the end of the month he was returned unopposed. It remained his seat for a few months short of thirty
years. His majorities were not always as big as he would have
liked, notably in 1923, his first election as Prime Minister,
when he rashly asked for 10,000 and got 6000; but he was
never in remote danger of losing the seat.

He was in his forty-first year when he entered the House of
Commons, six months over the watershed which Joseph
Chamberlain, thirty years before, had thought was the limit if a
fully effective parliamentary career was not to be precluded. He
was younger at entry than either his predecessor (Bonar Law)
or his successor (Neville Chamberlain) as leader of the
Conservative Party, but older, and in most cases significantly
so, than any other Prime Minister, of any party, of the past two
hundred years.

The House of Commons accepted him as a quiet, agreeable member of some substance, not the sort of man who would ever dominate in debate, or who would lead a school of thought, but a man who with three or four others might constitute a very effective block within his party to a course or an individual of which or whom they did not approve. Baldwin spoke very little – only five real speeches, interlaced with an occasional stray intervention, between his election in 1908 and the outbreak of war in 1914. Until then he appeared perfectly content with his placid existence. He had two substantial houses (in London he lived at 27 Queen's Gate until 1913, when he bought 93 Eaton Square, a still larger house with – an uncharacteristic touch for Baldwin – a more fashionable address) and plenty of money with which to run them and do anything else he wanted. He was vice-chairman of Baldwins Ltd and could get his way in the firm when he wished, without having to take full executive responsibility for what was becoming an increasingly large business. He had succeeded his father on the board of the Great Western Railway, although not in the chairmanship. He counted as a significant businessman on the Conservative benches. He had a growing circle of friends, almost entirely non-aristocratic, both in Worcestershire and in London, both inside and outside the House of Commons, and he entertained on a moderate scale. Being a backbench Member of Parliament rounded off his life rather than offering a springboard for future achievement. Lloyd George, Winston Churchill, F. E. Smith strove for the glittering prizes of politics. So, somewhat less rumbustiously, did Bonar Law and Austen Chamberlain.* Asquith and Balfour enjoyed them without the striving. Baldwin at this stage appeared to contemplate neither the strife nor the prizes.

The outbreak of war made him more restless. He was forty-seven, too old for military service yet young enough to feel that something more was required of him than the life he had hitherto led. At first the main change was that he began to give away quite a lot of money, mainly to Worcestershire charities.

Over a few years he disposed of about £40,000. Then he served on several Government committees of enquiry or review as well as engaging in a little more political manoeuvring than had been his habit. In the early part of the first coalition he was rather anti-Lloyd George and pro-Asquith, but by December 1916 he was ready for a change and accepted the pro-Lloyd George lead of Bonar Law, who had a little hesitantly made him his parliamentary private secretary a few months before. He was also ready for office, and was delighted when an offer came in the first few weeks of the new Government. It came in a rather strange form. Nominally he merely continued as parliamentary private secretary to Law at the Treasury. But Law was without a junior minister in the Commons. The new Financial Secretary was Sir Hardman Lever, a businessman brought in from outside politics to galvanize the Treasury. But as he was at first without a seat in Parliament and in any event left almost immediately for extended duty in the United States, he was unable either to galvanize or to discharge any of the traditional functions of his office. Quite exceptionally, there-fore, Baldwin was allowed to perform as a member of the Government and spoke from the front bench from February 1917 onwards. In July the position was regularized and he was given the title and salary of Joint Financial Secretary. He was a few weeks short of his fiftieth birthday, a somewhat elderly junior minister. But for the last two years of the war he at least had something to do.

CHAPTER TWO

The Leap to Fame

Baldwin remained Financial Secretary to the Treasury for four years. He served two Chancellors, Bonar Law in war and Austen Chamberlain in peace. He preferred Law, who was less stiff, although Chamberlain's more leisurely pace of work was better suited to Baldwin's own practice. Both of them regarded Baldwin as an acceptable and agreeable assistant, but not as a great deal more. He spent long hours in the House of Commons and he was skilful at the quiet conduct of minor business. Although it was recorded that 'he could read a balance sheet' (not in fact a particularly useful attribute for the Treasury), there is no evidence that he left any imprint upon Exchequer policy. Both his Chancellors – the two most important figures in the Conservative Party – thought of him, not as a man of promise, but as a man who deserved some reward by virtue of his service. In 1920 he was offered the Governor-Generalships, first of South Africa and then of Australia, together with a peerage. He declined. His name was also mooted for the Speakership of the House of Commons. It is not clear whether he was tempted or not, but the suggestion was not pressed. They were all offices which indicated that he was held in good regard, but not considered a serious candidate for major political advancement.*

Baldwin himself, however, had already raised his sights

---

* The only other future Prime Minister who was discussed for the Speakership was Campbell-Bannerman (in 1895), three years before he most unexpectedly became leader of the Liberal Party.

rather higher. At the time of Chamberlain's appointment he had written to his mother: 'I am pretty certain that I shall be left where I am which is what I wanted, for the only promotion I should care about would be the Exchequer itself which would never be given to a minister of only two years' experience. I anticipate that Austen will be my new chief, an appointment that will meet with a good deal of criticism.'[1] Baldwin's modesty, about which he wrote and spoke frequently, was not excessive.

The outside offices for which his name was subsequently canvassed were all posts in which Lloyd George took little interest. Baldwin, in the Coalition Government, was a moon who moved with and around the leader of the Conservative Party. With the Sun King himself he had little direct relationship. Of course he saw him occasionally, but rarely if ever alone. During 1918 they met principally at Lord Derby's• breakfasts, from which Baldwin recorded impressions and interchanges which indicate both that the Prime Minister was a near stranger to him and that he was not above a little daring toadying. On 4 March he wrote: '[The breakfasts] give me a good opportunity of studying that strange little genius who presides over us. He is an extraordinary compound.' And on 15 May, the morning of the Maurice• debate,* he recorded: 'We proceeded thus: S.B. – "You know, PM, that for ten years we have been trying to catch you deviating by an inch from the strict path of veracity and pin you down. We never succeeded. But now others think they have got you and they will find out this afternoon that they have caught you speaking the truth. They will have the shock of their lives." The little man roared with laughter and it evidently pleased him for he went about afterwards telling the Cabinet that "he had been caught telling the truth".'[2]

So indeed it might have pleased him, for as has subsequently

---

* This was one of the most crucial parliamentary occasions in Lloyd George's career. It is remarkable that he should have started the day by going out to a leisurely breakfast party.

become clear, the best that can be said about the debate, from the Prime Minister's point of view, is that he had one facet of the truth while General Maurice had another. But what is of greater Baldwin significance is the clear indication that at this stage he had developed little of the pervading antipathy towards Lloyd George which was to be the making of his own career.

Baldwin's most notable act as Financial Secretary was to write an anonymous letter to *The Times*. It appeared on 24 June 1919. It was of some length and contained a number of *obiter dicta* about the obvious gravity of the crisis through which the nation had passed, the less obvious but equally searching crisis which it still faced, the dangers of living in fools' paradises and believing that there could be play without work, the crushing burden of debt, and the responsibilities of the wealthy classes. A voluntary levy, he decided, was the answer. The operative part of his letter ran as follows:

> I have been considering this matter for nearly two years, but my mind moves slowly; I dislike publicity, and I had hoped that somebody else might lead the way. I have made as accurate an estimate as I am able of the value of my own estate, and have arrived at a total of about £580,000. I have decided to realise 20% of that amount or say £120,000 which will purchase £150,000 of the new War Loan, and present it to the Government for cancellation.
>
> I give this portion of my estate as a thank-offering in the firm conviction that never again shall we have such a chance of giving our country that form of help which is so vital at the present time.
>
> Yours, etc.
>
> F.S.T.

The gesture was generous and public spirited, with an element of naïveté about it. The anonymity (not perhaps best protected by the choice of pseudonym) held just long enough

for Baldwin to be alone in the secret amongst those present
when he performed his statutory Financial Secretary's duty
of witnessing the burning of the cancelled bonds, but not
for much longer. And the attempt to start an avalanche of
donations was a complete failure. Baldwin had aimed by his
example at a debt reduction of £1000 million. In the result only
about £½ million, including his own gift, was received.

Even more revealing of Baldwin's personality than *The Times*
letter and the action it announced was the note which he wrote
immediately afterwards to John Davidson,• who despite a
twenty-two-year age gap had become and was to remain one of
his closest friends:

> My dear old David,
> You and I and Miss Watson* have done it with a
> vengeance! I don't know what you said to *The Times*
> man, but when I opened the paper in bed (*ut mea mos
> est*) wondering whether my letter would find a place at
> all – well I dived under the bed clothes and went pink all
> over – as pink as you!
> I felt like a criminal in momentary fear of detection.
> But – remember this, *mon chou*. Next time you get a
> letter from me and feel inclined to belittle my style,
> remember that the leading journal of the world calls it
> *noble*. Put that in your pipe and smoke it! Bless you for
> all your kindness to me.
>
> F.S.T. (Ferdinando Smike Thompson)

This was one of the most interesting letters ever written by
Baldwin. It is 'an extraordinary compound', as he himself
wrote of the Prime Minister, although the elements and the
whole are as different from anything which could have eman-
ated from Lloyd George as it is possible to imagine. Baldwin's

* Davidson's secretary, who later worked for Baldwin in 10 Downing Street, and
was still there, promoted to preparing answers to parliamentary questions under
Neville Chamberlain but demoted to dealing with 'the post' under Churchill
(J. Colville, *The Fringes of Power*, page 124).

letter is arch. It is intimate. It is affectionate. It is sentimental. It is mock-modest. It is self-satisfied. It is funny in one place and cloying in another. It is a little embarrassing. It is the letter of a man who believed his own values were better than those of most others, but who wanted the reassurance of friendship, after which he strove a little officiously, for the fact that this was really so.

At the end of March 1921 Baldwin's long tenure of the Financial Secretaryship came to an end. He was promoted to be President of the Board of Trade and joined the Lloyd George Coalition Cabinet. But the event which caused his promotion also undermined the stability of the Cabinet which he joined. Bonar Law had resigned through ill-health. For all his limitations, Law was an extremely effective politician. He knew how to hold the Conservative Party together, and, so long as he judged this right, to hold it loyal to Lloyd George. Austen Chamberlain, who succeeded him, had little skill in party leadership. He was aloof and wooden in dealings with his followers. His loyalty to Lloyd George and the idea of coalition was more complete than that of Law. But it was of less value. It was unconditional and therefore unrepresentative loyalty. To an increasing extent the leading Conservative members of the Cabinet, not only Chamberlain himself, but Birkenhead,• Curzon• and Horne• (who succeeded as Chancellor), and even Balfour as well, came to represent practically nobody but themselves. Meanwhile the post-war boom gave way to mounting and menacing unemployment, while the rootlessness of Lloyd George's policies, both at home and abroad, became increasingly apparent to those who were undazzled by his personality.

Baldwin was good at being undazzled. Throughout his nineteen months at the Board of Trade his principal public service was that of observing the Prime Minister with an increasingly jaundiced eye. He noted 'the disintegrating effect of Lloyd George on all with whom he had to deal' and came to regard him as 'a real corrupter of public life'. He saw this corruption as affecting ministers, the civil service and the House of Commons. He regarded the Prime Minister's unfastidious use of the honours system as the most obviously shocking but by no means necessarily the most dangerous manifestation of the system. What worried him most, apart from the meretricious glitter of the whole charade, was the erosion of the proper rôle of Cabinet Ministers, both in relation to their own departments and in their right to be fully consulted on matters of collective responsibility; the Prime Minister's indifference to the processes and opinions of the House of Commons, provided a majority would sustain him in office; and the disarray and poor morale which coalition under a dynamic chief of another party was creating in the headquarters and local organizations of the Conservative Party.

Lloyd George never appreciated the potential menace of Baldwin. He had put him in the Cabinet because, with Bonar Law gone, he needed a man from the Law stable to preserve the balance. But having put him in, he rarely consulted him on general policy issues and gave him little rôle even in industrial disputes, which were still the traditional concern of the Board of Trade. He commented patronisingly that almost the only sounds he heard from Baldwin during Cabinets were the rhythmic sucking of his pipe. He did not realize that each suck marked an extra notch of disapproval, a further step towards the precipice of his own irrevocable downfall.

Nineteen twenty-two was from the beginning an uneasy year for the Coalition. There was a continuing Conservative fear through the winter and spring months that Chamberlain and Birkenhead would be seduced by Lloyd George into agreeing to a snap election, and that the rest of the party would be confronted with a *fait accompli*, highly damaging whichever way they decided to play it. Then in June the honours scandal passed from the baroque to the rococo stage. With an ill-fated exuberance which only a government in its last stages could achieve, Lloyd George succeeded in assembling five nominations for peerages, four of which were alleged to be

discreditable. One, Sir Joseph Robinson, who had been con-
victed for fraudulent share-dealing in South Africa, was sufficiently so that the Chief Whip, F. E. Guest, was charged with
calling on him in his suite at the Savoy Hotel and telling him
that he had no alternative but to withdraw from the list even
though his name had already been published.* Robinson lost
his peerage and Lloyd George was forced to concede a Royal
Commission on future honours procedure, but the damage to
the Coalition could not be retrieved. The session ended with an
extraordinary meeting demanded by the Conservative junior
ministers in order that they might express their discontent to
the Cabinet members of their own party. Austen Chamberlain
stiffly told them that the meeting was unprecedented and
irregular, but it was left to Birkenhead to denounce them all for
impertinence, stupidity and disloyalty.

Baldwin watched in silence as the remarkable gathering
ground towards its angry conclusion. He spent most of August
in Worcestershire and September at Aix, which he had discovered the previous summer. During his first two weeks in
France he read no English newspaper and barely glanced at a
French one. But although his mind was detached from day-to-
day events it brooded a good deal on longer-term considera-
tions. He decided he had had enough of the Coalition. He
would break with Lloyd George, and it would remain to be seen
whether the victim would be himself or the Prime Minister.

The Chanak crisis,† which erupted in late September, drove

---

* At first (being a little hard of hearing) Robinson apparently assumed that he
was being asked for more money, beyond the £30,000 he was thought to have paid,
and compliantly drew out his cheque book. (John Campbell, *F. E. Smith*, pages
599–600.)
† The 1920 Treaty of Sèvres between the Allies and Turkey demilitarized the
Dardanelles and gave a zone around Smyrna to the Greeks. In August 1922 the
resurgent Turkish nationalists of Kemal Ataturk threw the Greeks into the sea,
reoccupied Smyrna and advanced north to Chanak, where they threatened the Straits
and menacingly confronted a small British force which represented the Allies. The
British Government was willing to negotiate a frontier rectification in favour of the
Turks, but not to yield to force – a reasonable enough position. However, the Prime
Minister (who was inclined to identify the Greeks with the Welsh), Churchill and
Birkenhead, supported by Austen Chamberlain and Robert Horne, were held by most
of the rest of the Cabinet, by Bonar Law from outside, and by the weight of Tory

Baldwin to the newsstands of Aix for the first time. Mrs Baldwin recorded what then happened (and also provided some insight into their life at Aix):

> I tried to persuade him that things couldn't be so bad as the French paper made out or he would have been wired for. The next day he went for a long walk, about 20 miles, during which he did a good deal of clear thinking in the mountains. The next day he and I went for a shorter walk and returned about 6. I was a little tired and went to my room to rest before dressing for dinner and he sat down to a game of Patience. Suddenly S. entered my room with a telegram in his hand saying: 'It has come. I have been expecting it. There is some devilment afoot and I must get back to back up poor dear old Austen'*. . . . It was decided that he should leave next day for London and that I should stop on and finish my baths and meet him in Paris.[3]

Baldwin reached London in time for a Cabinet on the morning of 1 October. This provided an occasion for him to develop his new-found resolve. He came out firmly for caution and against the Turkish adventure which was exciting Lloyd George, Churchill, Birkenhead and most of the other ardent Coalitionists. But this was not enough to secure a break, particularly as an armistice with Turkey was fairly quickly obtained. The more divisive issue was the old question of an election under united Coalition leadership. Chamberlain pro-

---

* In fact he did nothing of the sort, for he found 'poor dear old Austen' firmly on the wrong side.

---

backbench opinion to have behaved with unnecessary and irresponsible bellicosity. The split with almost uncanny precision thus ran along the line which was to divide the Coalitionists from the anti-Coalitionists as sharply as the British were divided from the Turks at Chanak. Curzon sat on the barbed wire on both issues, although he was later to achieve a great diplomatic triumph at Lausanne, where he unexpectedly secured a freely negotiated agreement with the Turks. This Conference of Lausanne, which lasted from November 1922 to February 1923, was notable not only for securing the demilitarization of the Straits but also for providing the circumstances out of which Harold Nicolson wrote his supremely funny essay *Arketall*.

posed this at a meeting of the Conservative ministers on 10 October. At this stage Baldwin alone dissented strongly. It was by far the most resolute action of his political life up to that point. He had nudged his way at Aix into an instinctive decision about the correct course to follow but he was agreeably shocked by his own daring in following it. Lucy Baldwin did not return to England until 12 October. Their plan for a Paris *rendez-vous* had collapsed. Baldwin then went to meet her at Victoria Station and walked the half mile to their Eaton Square house with her, describing, as she subsequently wrote to her husband's mother, what had happened, in slightly breathless terms:

> I have done something dreadful without consulting you. I do hope you won't mind. I have been fearfully worried, but I felt that it had to come. I am resigning from the Cabinet. I shall never get a job again. I do hope you won't mind fearfully, but I've said I cannot continue to serve under the G* any longer.

He then described the development of the Turkish situation and continued:

> And then at a Cabinet meeting of Unionist Ministers it was decided to have the General Election and go to the country at once (without consulting any of the party) under the L.G. banner as Coalitionists. I arose and spoke and told them that I could not and would not do it. I must be free and stand as a Conservative; I could not serve under L.G. again. The rest of the Unionist Ministers were aghast and they were all apparently against me. At the next meeting of the Unionist Cabinet Ministers Boscawen• threw in his lot with me. Curzon was sympathetic, but that was all. So there it is. They will follow the G and I can't, so it means I shall drop out of politics altogether.[4]

* Abbreviation for 'the Goat', as Lloyd George was unflatteringly referred to by some of his less friendly colleagues.

Baldwin's pessimism about the future was probably genuine, although totally misplaced. At any rate he took it sufficiently seriously to be anxious to resign and retreat to Worcestershire immediately, without waiting to see what forces might crystallize around him, and to make tentative plans for spending the winter abroad. In fact his position was very strong, and predictably so. The Coalition was not really a confluence of parties. It was Lloyd George pirouetting on the large base of the Conservative Party. And the overwhelming part of the base was tired of the dance. Baldwin had the support of the Chief Whip (Leslie Wilson)*; the Chairman of the Party (Younger•); the Chief Agent; Salisbury• and Derby, the Party's two principal territorial magnates, although the latter as always was a little hesitant; the majority of Conservative junior ministers; a substantial but uncounted number of backbenchers; and the editor of *The Times*.† As a team with which to go goat-hunting it was not quite so exiguous as he implied.

What he thought he needed was someone with the public fame to take over the leadership and to hold a candle to the great names of Lloyd George, Austen Chamberlain, Churchill, Birkenhead and Balfour. He could not at that stage hope to fulfil this rôle himself. There seemed only one man who could, and that was Bonar Law, his fragile health somewhat improved as a result of eighteen months out of the Government, and his loyalty to Lloyd George and Austen Chamberlain weakened by the same cause. The great issue of the next week was whether Law could agree to attend the Carlton Club meeting which Chamberlain had summoned at short notice for the Thursday morning, 19 October. Everything was held to depend on this. And when, as late as the Wednesday morning, Law announced that, as the doctors had passed him as fit for only two years,

* The Coalition had joint Chief Whips as did the Churchill Coalition twenty years later. Wilson (1876–1955), MP for Reading (1913–22) and Portsmouth South (1922–3), then Governor of Bombay (1923–8), was Conservative Whip; F. E. Guest (see page 48 *supra*), 1875–1937, third son of the 1st Lord Wimborne and first cousin of Churchill, was Liberal Whip.

† Henry Wickham Steed (1871–1956). His brief editorship (1919–22) was an interval between the two spans of Geoffrey Robinson (later Dawson, *q.v.*).

he could not accept the rôle which attendance implied, the Baldwin forces were sunk in gloom.

It is difficult not to believe that they attached too much importance to Law's availability. His reputation amongst Conservative Members of Parliament was high. But his advice was not in doubt, only whether he would lead the independent appeal to the country. No doubt his electoral leadership was of value; but can it have been of decisive importance? He was a sad knight in slightly drooping armour. Those who regarded his attendance as vital were probably taken in too much by the spirit of Birkenhead's subsequent jibe about cabin boys taking over captains' jobs. When captains become as distrusted as Lloyd George and Birkenhead himself, crews would rather see almost anyone else in charge.

In the event there was no test of what would have happened in Bonar Law's absence. On the Wednesday evening he decided that he would attend. Thursday morning's newspapers were dominated by this news, accompanied by that of the victory of an independent (i.e. anti-Coalition) Conservative candidate in a by-election at Newport. But Thursday morning's meeting was dominated not by Law but by Baldwin. Austen Chamberlain began with a half-hour lecture on behalf of the majority of the Conservative members of the Cabinet. Baldwin spoke for eight minutes on behalf of the minority. It was a beautifully judged speech. He had to combat Chamberlain's appeal for loyalty to his own leadership. He did it by counterposing the need for regard to the greater entity of the Conservative Party. He dealt extremely gently with Chamberlain, who was present and still respected, reserving the edge of his debating power entirely for Lloyd George, who was absent and distrusted:

> [The Prime Minister] is a dynamic force, and it is from that very fact that our troubles, in our opinion, arise. A dynamic force is a very terrible thing; it may crush you but it is not necessarily right. It is owing to that dynamic

force, and that remarkable personality, that the Liberal Party, to which he formerly belonged, has been smashed to pieces; and it is my firm conviction that, in time, the same thing will happen to our party. I do not propose to elaborate, in an assembly like this, the dangers and the perils of that happening. . . . I think that if the present association is continued, and if this meeting agrees that it should be continued, you will see some more breaking up, and I believe the process must go on inevitably until the old Conservative Party is smashed to atoms and lost in ruins.

I would like to give you just one illustration to show what I mean by the disintegrating influence of a dynamic force. Take Mr Chamberlain and myself. Mr Chamberlain's services to the State are infinitely greater than any I have been able to render, but we are both men who are giving all we can give to the service of the State; we are both men who are, or try to be, actuated by principle in our conduct; we are men who, I think, have exactly the same views on the political problems of the day; we are men who I believe – certainly on my side – have esteem and perhaps I may say affection for each other; but the result of this dynamic force is that we stand here today, he prepared to go into the wilderness if he should be compelled to forsake the Prime Minister, and I prepared to go into the wilderness if I should be compelled to stay with him. If that is the effect of that tremendous personality on two men occupying the position that we do, and related to each other in the way that Mr Chamberlain and I are, that process must go on throughout the party. It was for that reason that I took the stand I did, and put forward the views that I did. I do not know what the majority here or in the country may think about it. I said at the time what I thought was right, and I stick all through to what I believe to be right.

The effect was dramatic. Baldwin received an enthusiastic reception. It was the first of many speeches in which by the measured and skilful deployment of moderate words he visibly affected the opinions of a crucial audience. The debate proceeded. A motion to withdraw support from the Coalition was moved by a senior Essex backbencher.* Bonar Law added a few effective but unremembered sentences at the end. The motion was then carried by 185 to 88.†

That afternoon Lloyd George resigned. Bonar Law waited to be confirmed as leader at a full Hotel Cecil party meeting on the Monday before accepting the King's commission. His strength was as a representative figure, not as an 'independent statesman' like those whose advice had been swept aside at the Carlton Club, and he wished this to be underlined by a meticulous attention to proper procedure. This did not prevent his offering Baldwin the Exchequer before he had kissed hands. Baldwin undoubtedly wanted the job. He had done so four years before, and nothing had happened in the meantime either to abate his ambition or to make him less qualified – in the latter case very much the reverse. Furthermore, the offer could hardly have been a surprise to him. He had done more than anyone else to make the new Government.

Yet he declined. He suggested that Reginald McKenna,• Asquith's last Chancellor, who was currently out of Parliament and chairman of the Midland Bank, should be approached instead. Law accepted the suggestion. McKenna took three days to consider the offer before refusing, nominally on health grounds. Law called on Baldwin with the news. Baldwin then accepted the post and was very pleased with himself. He went upstairs to his wife and said: 'Treat me with respect; I am the Chancellor of the Exchequer.'

* Ernest Pretyman (1860–1931), MP for Woodbridge (1895–1906) and Chelmsford (1908–23).

† Only MPs were invited to speak or vote in the meeting although some peers attended, including Birkenhead, whose late arrival during Austen Chamberlain's speech was greeted by a cry of 'traitor', which Chamberlain mistakenly thought was intended for him.

His *nolo episcopari* phase cannot be easily explained. At the end of the day he got exactly what he wanted – high office, achieved not merely without push but with a positive and recorded show of reluctance. Yet a cynical explanation does not stand up. He could not possibly have been confident that McKenna would refuse: the former Chancellor's three days of hesitation is proof against this. It is difficult to reject the view that he was genuinely anxious, first not to appear to profit from his own actions in bringing about the downfall of the Coalition, and second to strengthen the new Government, which he thought, probably mistakenly, that McKenna would do.

The new Government needed strength, for without Austen Chamberlain, Balfour, Birkenhead or Horne it looked weak on paper, and it had to face an immediate general election. The result was a substantial triumph. The Conservatives won an overall majority of ninety, with the opposition split into three factions, but the Labour Party much stronger than either the Asquithian or the Lloyd George Liberals. Baldwin's most notable contribution to the campaign was to exploit Lloyd George's remark that Bonar Law was 'honest to the verge of simplicity'. 'By God,' he commented, 'that is what we have been looking for.'

The election won, Baldwin prepared to move, both into 11 Downing Street, which was his by right, and into Chequers, which Bonar Law did not want. Eaton Square was sold. It was a correct decision. He was to spend most of the next fourteen years in official residences.

Baldwin's Chancellorship was notable principally for his American debt settlement. This was one of the most tangled of post-1918 issues. It involved the questions of reparations from Germany, Britain's claims on her European allies, her credit in the United States, and the possibility of American help towards stabilisation in Europe – the German economy being sunk in inflationary disarray. Furthermore Baldwin had to negotiate against the background of a damaging partial commitment by the Coalition Government, including the elegantly drafted but ill-judged Balfour note of July 1922, and an American public opinion which was inward-looking and brashly commercial. 'They hired the money, didn't they?' was a simpler appeal than intricate arguments about Britain's countervailing claims, the difference between a war debt and a normal commercial transaction, and the problems (however vividly exemplified by Germany) of making large payments across the exchanges without upsetting international trade. Still greater than these difficulties was Bonar Law's stubborn (and in many ways sensible) resolve not to accept a massive continuing burden. He had said that he regarded all-round cancellation as the only fair solution to inter-Allied debts, and this remained his basic position throughout. Reluctantly, however, he authorised Baldwin to make a settlement which did not exceed a payment of £25 million a year.

Baldwin's mission to Washington took him away from 27 December to 27 January. There were fluctuating negotiations, and some acerbity in the flow of telegrams from London. 'Is it not possible that you are too much under the influence of Washington which is not even the New York atmosphere?'[5] In spite of such warnings Baldwin's desire for a settlement was fortified by the views of the Governor of the Bank of England, Montagu Norman,• who was with him, and of Auckland Geddes,• the 'political' Ambassador in Washington. Baldwin tabled proposals which involved payments of £34 million a year. The Americans countered by accepting this for the first ten years, but adding an extra ½ per cent interest, bringing the annual figure to £40 million for the remaining fifty-two years.

Baldwin thought the counter-offer acceptable, but as a rump Cabinet of the Prime Minister and six other members unanimously rejected it, he was forced to return with the matter unconcluded. At Southampton he made his own posi-tion devastatingly clear to the waiting journalists. He disclosed the terms of the American offer, he left no doubt that they were in his opinion the best that could be obtained and should be accepted, and he rounded things off with what were interpreted as some highly uncomplimentary remarks about the quality of the Congressional opinion which had to be accommodated.

There then ensued one of the most extraordinary episodes in the history of British Cabinet government. There was no discussion between the Prime Minister and the Chancellor for two days. Then they together met the American Ambassador. Law denounced the proposed settlement. Baldwin remained silent. But he defended his attitude firmly at the Cabinet on the same day. The Prime Minister argued against him, and when opinion swung heavily in the Chancellor's favour he indicated that he would resign rather than accept the settlement. An adjournment was then agreed to. The next morning (30 January) *The Times* carried an anonymous letter, rather quaintly signed 'Colonial', which repeated several of the arguments and phrases used by Law the previous afternoon. It was in fact written by the Prime Minister.

That same morning the entire Cabinet, with the exception of the Prime Minister, met in the Lord Chancellor's room. Only Lord Novar,• the Scottish Secretary, was in favour of repudiating the Baldwin settlement. A deputation of Baldwin, the Lord Chancellor (Cave•) and the Duke of Devonshire• was appointed to wait upon Bonar Law and persuade him not to resign. Law agreed, although not with a very good grace. He had discovered that City opinion, for the interpretation of which he relied upon McKenna and which he had previously been informed was strongly against acceptance, had swung overwhelmingly in favour. The terms were endorsed at a five-minute Cabinet that afternoon.

Not surprisingly, neither Law's relations with Baldwin nor his authority in the Government ever fully recovered from these incidents. Beaverbrook, indeed, who knew Law very well but was also addicted to dramatic interpretations, believed that the collapse of Law's health stemmed partly from this destruction of his position as undisputed captain, maybe of 'the second eleven' in Churchill's phrase, but at least of a team of like-minded, straightforward and loyal men. And there is some indication that Baldwin, from this time forward, felt that he was dealing with a time-expired Prime Minister. He began to flex his political muscles.

The first overt expression of this came in a House of Commons speech on 16 February, replying to a Labour amendment in the debate on the Address. He ranged far wide of any possible Treasury brief or of the broadest interpretation of his Exchequer responsibilities. He replied to MacDonald and Lloyd George. He discussed the basis of the Government's foreign policy as well as the debt settlement and unemployment. He envisaged not the possibility but the certainty of a Labour Government – 'when the Labour Party sit on these benches'. And he ended with a homily, trite or profound according to taste.

> Four words, of one syllable each, are words which contain salvation for this country and for the whole world, and they are faith, hope, love and work. No Government in this country today which has not faith in the future, love for its fellow-men, and which will not work and work and work will ever bring this country through into better days and better times, or will ever bring Europe through, or the world through.[6]

It was the first of a whole series of his ruminative House of Commons orations, at once homespun and high-flown, which, whatever else may be thought about them, rarely failed to capture the ears of his listeners. Even more notably it was the speech, not of a subordinate minister, but of a leader, striking a new note, and invoking an enthusiastic response from a broad segment of the electorate.

Baldwin's next major public appearance was his Budget speech in April. It was a dull Budget, but not a dull speech. Almost its only significant proposal was concerned with debt management and the creation of a new sinking fund. But the speech was brief and unplatitudinous and earned many compliments. It did nothing to impair his rising reputation. This was important, for Bonar Law's health was on the point of finally breaking up. On 1 May he left for a Mediterranean cruise in the vain hope that this might cause an improvement. It did not. He had cancer of the throat, and on 19 May, too ill to go to Buckingham Palace, he resigned by letter.

The drama of the succession, whether it should go to Curzon or to Baldwin, has always been treated as one of the great hair's-breadth decisions of British constitutional history. In retrospect, however, it is difficult to see how, unless the King had shown most remarkable misjudgment, it could have been decided other than it was. No doubt there was room for argument as to whether in 1923 it was still possible to have a peer as Conservative Prime Minister. It was only twenty-one years since Salisbury had concluded his long and successful period of power, and only twenty-eight years since another peer (Rosebery) had presided (although less successfully) over a Liberal Government. And no doubt it needed Balfour's subtle reasoning* to convince the King of this *constitutional* point, particularly as there were others – Salisbury, for example – strongly urging the claims of Curzon.

The constitutional point, however, was by no means the only one at issue. There was also the personal one. Curzon had a long record of devoted although doubtfully successful public service. He was a weak man, and in some ways a slightly ridiculous one. Davidson, who was of course a committed partisan of Baldwin's, but a sufficiently skilful one to couch his arguments in moderate terms, probably got nearest to the nub of Curzon's failings in a memorandum which he wrote for Stamfordham• and through him for the King. After beginning by saying that the case for either candidate was 'very strong' and paying a tribute to Curzon's long experience, he continued:

* He was asked, as a disinterested elder statesman and former Conservative Prime Minister, to come to London and see the King on the afternoon of Whit Monday (22 May). When he returned to the house at Sheringham in Norfolk where he was staying he was asked by old mutual friends, 'And will dear George [Curzon] be chosen?' 'No,' he replied with feline Balfourian satisfaction, 'dear George will not.' (K. Rose, *Superior Person*, page 383.)

On the other hand, there can be no doubt that Lord Curzon, temperamentally, does not inspire complete confidence in his colleagues, either as to his judgment or as to his ultimate strength of purpose in a crisis. His methods, too, are inappropriate to harmony. The prospect of his receiving deputations as Prime Minister from the Miners' Federation or the Triple Alliance, for example, is capable of causing alarm for the future relations between the Government and Labour – between moderate and less moderate opinion.[7]

Furthermore, Curzon's behaviour over the fall of the Co-alition was fresh in men's minds and had made him a lot of enemies and few friends. He took no stand, but resigned at the last moment from the Lloyd George Cabinet so as to be in-gratiatingly available to continue as Foreign Secretary in the new Government. The truth of the matter was that there were very few who wanted him as Prime Minister, independently of the House of Lords issue. The Cabinet did not, the party machine did not, the constituencies did not, at least three quarters of the Conservative members of the House of Commons did not. An exception was Salisbury, the leader of the diehards, who, like Balfour, was specially consulted by the King. Another half-exception may have been Bonar Law. He refused on grounds of health to tender any formal advice. But he saw Baldwin on the Sunday morning and told him that he had no doubt that Curzon would be chosen, although his own turn would come in due course. Then, when pressed by his principal private secretary, Colonel Waterhouse,• he reluc-tantly said that if he had to advise, 'he would put Baldwin first'. Waterhouse, probably improperly, passed this information on to the Palace. Then on the Monday morning Law saw Salisbury and left him with the impression that Curzon could not be 'passed over'. The likelihood is that he saw the decisive dis-advantages of Curzon but could not quite reconcile himself to the thought of the very junior Baldwin, who had so recently 'bounced' and damaged him over the debt settlement, being in 10 Downing Street.

Compared with the strong forces and arguments working the other way all this counted for little. Curzon was in fact impossible. He could only have been chosen had there been no other credible candidate, and Baldwin's performance from the date of the Carlton Club meeting forward had destroyed this possibility. The well-known story of Curzon's Tuesday summons from Montacute* to London, of his confident and much-photographed arrival, first at Paddington Station and then at Carlton House Terrace, followed by the crushing blow delivered to him that afternoon when Stamfordham called at his house and told him Baldwin was to be Prime Minister, was not therefore a sudden snatching from his hands of the steadily earned and well-deserved prize, but more the last rather over-dramatized act of a tragi-comedy which had been played out in varying forms since his appointment as Viceroy of India in 1898.†

---

* A late sixteenth-century house beyond Yeovil, Somerset, which Curzon could not resist acquiring on a long lease despite the fact that he was already renting Hackwood, near Basingstoke, and, after the death of his father in 1916, owned Kedleston in Derbyshire. He was a great improver of all his properties, even removing a small hill at Hackwood so that the view should be less impeded.

† Since first drafting this passage I have read Kenneth Rose's excellent 1983 biography of King George V. I think he would contest at least the emphasis of what I have written. Such at any rate would seem to follow from his summing-up sentence: 'The King had preferred Baldwin to Curzon for one reason alone: that he sat in the House of Commons' (page 273). But I am not convinced that there is necessarily a conflict. The King knew Curzon much better than he knew Baldwin, and no doubt did not wish to wound him unnecessarily. It therefore suited well to fasten firmly on the objective House of Commons point. It might have been regarded as much less conclusive had the peer under consideration been preferred on merits by the King and by the generality of Conservative opinion. And indeed the King went out of his way to make it clear that he was not laying down a rule against a House of Lords Prime Minister for the future: 'What I said was that there were circumstances in which it was very undesirable that a peer should be Prime Minister and in my view this was such a case' (Rose, pages 272–3). One of the circumstances was perhaps the fact that the Government was already very strongly represented in the House of Lords. Another, in my view probably more important, was the personality and character of the two contenders. Seventeen years later, when a similar issue arose between Churchill and Halifax (except that Halifax was not a contender), the latter was certainly not automatically excluded because of his membership of the House of Lords, although once again it was a fortunate contributory factor.

Baldwin had spent the weekend partly in London and partly at Chequers. On the Saturday evening, before seeing Law on the following morning, he dined with Davidson at the Argentine Club and informed him that he would 'rather take a single ticket to Siberia than become Prime Minister'.[8] Davidson, who was used to him, did not take this seriously, and rightly so, for Baldwin's next railway activity was to leave Chequers early on the Tuesday morning in order to catch the 8.55 from Wendover and be available to see first Stamfordham and then the King. Stamfordham asked him if he would be prepared to retain Curzon as Foreign Secretary. He said that he would welcome this, but queried whether Curzon would be willing to serve, and also indicated that he would endeavour to bring Austen Chamberlain and Horne back into the Government. These replies were highly satisfactory to the King, who summoned Baldwin to the Palace at 3.15 p.m. and charged him with the task of forming a Government.

He returned to Downing Street and asked the waiting journalists for their prayers rather than their congratulations. He was Prime Minister at fifty-five, after less than three years' Cabinet experience. He wrote to his mother: 'I am not a bit excited and don't realize it in the least.' But to Phyllis Broome, a Worcestershire neighbour, writer and walking companion, he wrote: 'Here is the biggest job in the world and if I fail I shall share the fate of many a bigger man than I. But it's a fine thought, isn't it? And one may do something before one cracks up.'[9]

CHAPTER THREE

An Unsettled Leadership

Baldwin of course did not 'crack up' for many years to come. He held the leadership of the Conservative Party, to which he was unanimously elected (proposed by Curzon) immediately following his accession to the premiership, until 1937, a longer period than any of his predecessors since Salisbury, and a longer period too than any but one (Churchill) of his seven successors has since attained.

Yet the suggestion of 'crack-up' was not wholly fanciful. A bucolic English gentleman 'by election', in G. M. Young's• phrase, he was always very highly strung. He was full of minor nervous habits: an eye-twitch, a frequent snapping of the thumbs and fingers when reading or in conversation, a flicking of the tongue before starting a speech, and, in a rather different category, an addiction to putting objects, particularly books, but matches, pipes, paper knives and almost anything else as well, to his nostrils and audibly sniffing at them.

More importantly, he had a metabolism which reacted strongly to crisis. He performed well but not easily during periods of strain. He then slept badly and became more silent and withdrawn than was his habit. But his power of decision-making improved, and his gift of calming, persuasive oratory rose to its heights. After such a period he was left exhausted, sometimes near to nervous prostration. But a long holiday would revive him quickly: if he had the prospect of a month of freedom he would began to feel well after a week or so.

As a result he was good at crises provided they did not occur frequently. He enjoyed the aftermath of a successful battle. He did not want the next one to start soon. He had no desire to defeat boredom by provoking political excitement and keeping himself constantly at a stretch. He was mostly happy without an excessive amount of work, and when it was not there he did not invent it. It is not altogether easy to understand his methods of discharging business. The charge of simple laziness can be dismissed. Had this been his dominating characteristic, he could not possibly have retained his position through the vicissitudes and challenges of a decade and a half. Nor was he like Asquith, whose urbane liberal gravitas he greatly admired, and who, of all the leading politicians he knew, was probably the one he would have most wished to emulate. Asquith worked with unusual speed and intellectual certainty. He operated, in Churchill's view, like a great judge. He listened to the pleadings. He absorbed the arguments. He gave his verdict. And then he closed the court and turned his mind and his emotions to the pleasures of the day, literary or social.

Baldwin had no comparable speed, no comparable rational processes. Tom Jones,• one of his most intimate associates and normally a very shrewd observer, at first thought him very slow. 'Bonar Law would do as much work in an hour as S.B. in four or five,' he wrote in November 1923.[1] He also noted that Baldwin would rather walk and gossip, or withdraw for a Sunday evening to sit alone with Mrs Baldwin, than work on Cabinet papers or even a speech. What he did not realise at that stage was that it was meaningless to compare Baldwin's speed with that of Bonar Law, for Baldwin did not work at all in Law's sense. Law was a highly efficient, rather unimaginative, detailed administrator, given political force by a strong sense of partisan combativeness. He worked on paper, and derived a sense of duty fulfilled as he proceeded through his Cabinet boxes. He ran a Department of State with the detailed application which he had devoted to making his way in Glasgow business.

Baldwin never attempted to do this. He was not afraid of

Wilden House

The Baldwins on their honeymoon

Astley Hall: Baldwin's Worcestershire
house from 1902

Alfred Baldwin outside the House of Commons, c. 1900

Stanley Baldwin outside the House of Commons, 1909

Baldwin at Aix-les-Bains, August 1923 (left to right: Lucy Baldwin, SB, Mimi Davidson, John Davidson)

Lord Curzon judges the joggers, Baldwin and Bruce (of Australia); Smuts (South Africa) and Mackenzie King (Canada) remain more static. Imperial Conference, 1923

Austen Chamberlain informally dressed for luncheon with
his constituents, Birmingham, 1922

A solid centre with tentative flanks: Baldwin with Tom Jones
(on his right) and his second son, Windham (later 3rd Earl)
Baldwin, Astley, 1923

A concert party for the colonials? Prince of Wales and
Prime Minister in Canada, 1927. Mrs Baldwin is between them;
Prince George, later Duke of Kent, is on Baldwin's right

Prime Minister and private secretary: Baldwin and
Sir Ronald Waterhouse during the General Strike

Oliver Baldwin MP (Lab.), 1929

A rich top table: Birkenhead, Baldwin, Edgar Wallace, Fleuriau (French Ambassador) and Churchill at a Press Club luncheon, c. 1927

overall responsibility. Indeed, for the first three months of his premiership he performed a feat which had seemed remarkable even when Gladstone had last done it forty years before and retained the Chancellorship as well as being First Lord of the Treasury. But it was all done on a light rein and with the minimum of paperwork. He did not even pretend to a crushing burden of work, only enough to complain comfortably about. 'The work goes on, one week like another, and pretty incessant until Friday night, and then the break which gives one time to get one's breath again,' he wrote to his mother two months after becoming Prime Minister. 'So far . . . it is not too heavy. . . . When you are at the beck and call of everyone for 14 hours a day for four days and for 8 hours on the fifth day each week you want a short space in which you relax and do just what you like.'[2] All subsequent Prime Ministers would, I think, have regarded a sixty-four-hour week which closed at 5 p.m. on Friday as a semi-holiday.

He was able to achieve this amount of leisure because he did not intervene much in the work of the Departments. Partly as a reaction against the restless interference of Lloyd George, he believed in giving his ministers the maximum freedom. He was always available for consultation, but rarely forced it upon them.

He devoted a lot of time to the personal relationships of politics and to conducting them in a mollifying, unhurried way. This took priority over the reading of briefs, the annotation of Cabinet papers, or the swift making of minor decisions. This was not a question of either niceness or laziness. It was a question of how he believed he could best attain his major political purposes. This practice extended far beyond the circle of his Cabinet colleagues. It led him to spend endless hours in the House of Commons, far more than any Prime Minister for many years before, far more than any of his successors. Sometimes he would merely sit on the Government bench, half listening to some minor debate, half wrapping his mind round the backgrounds and appearances of different members. Then he would use this information to chat knowledgeably and sympathetically to them in the lobbies or the smoking room, often concentrating as much upon the opposition as upon his own supporters.* Sometimes he just sat. 'What can you do', an exasperated colleague once complained, 'with a leader who sits in the smoking room reading the *Strand Magazine*?'[3]

The interesting point is not the seeming indolence but the subject matter and the *venue*. Asquith would never have chosen the *Strand Magazine* or the House of Commons as a place in which to read. He would have read more reconditely but equally haphazardly in some more private precinct. Churchill in office would never have wasted time in the smoking room without an audience. Lloyd George would never have wasted time there at all, but he might have chosen the *Strand Magazine* had he been left waiting upon a railway platform. Neville Chamberlain would never have read haphazardly. Ramsay MacDonald would never have exposed himself so apparently free from the burdens of state.

Yet it is doubtful whether Baldwin was in fact wasting time. He was most likely not even reading the *Strand*, but sniffing it and with it the atmosphere around him. He was also probably ruminating, feeling his way, nudging towards a variety of decisions which he had to make. This was a technique which made it peculiarly difficult to say when he was working and when he was not. It made his work pattern not merely different from but the opposite to that of Asquith. With him the courts were rarely wholly open and never, except occasionally at Aix, wholly shut. His desk application was poor, but his recreations were semi-political. This was true of his walks, of his quiet dinners at the Davidsons' or in the Travellers' Club, of his afternoons of reading or letter-writing. He was contemptuous of those who could think and talk of nothing but party politics and political careers, but his own talk (and presumably his own

---

* I recall being told how, in my father's first few months as a Labour member in 1935, Baldwin stopped him beside the open fire which then burned in the 'no' division lobby and talked for a quarter of an hour or more about his own experiences as a young man on visits to the tinplate mills of my father's Monmouthshire constituency.

thought) was much about the penumbra of government and the idiosyncrasies of politicians. Lloyd George, in particular, was an unfailing source of repellent fascination to him.

An inordinate proportion of his time was devoted to speech preparation and delivery. This was not because he was over-meticulous with individual words or phrases. Indeed, in the House of Commons and even in his highly expert use of the new medium of broadcasting, he often eschewed a manuscript and spoke from relatively sketchy notes. But he devoted a great deal of prior thought to the mood which he wished to create.* It was in this way that he made many of his policy decisions. A major speech had to be delivered. He wished its effect to be that of edging his audience and the nation in a particular direction. Accordingly, any policy announced had to be compatible with the objective. Any specific proposals, however, almost always followed from the mood and the words used to assist it, rather than first being sharply worked out, and then sustained by *ex post* argument. Baldwin was not in the highest category of orators. He had a good speaking voice, he was persuasive, he could mostly secure the attention of his opponents. He rarely opened new vistas and he rarely inspired his supporters. It was more that he carried them reluctantly with him. Yet to an exceptional extent the turning points of his career were marked not by actions but by speeches. He was right to devote a lot of attention to them.

These turning points apart, he was also an addictive non-political speaker. He could seldom resist an invitation to address a learned society, a university, a county or regional association, a professional body, indeed any gathering of apparently public-spirited gentlemen brought together for non-commercial purposes. These speeches had to be rich in

---

* He described his method of approaching a speech in a letter to Davidson written a couple of years later: 'I just want a quiet morning to think . . . it is just getting that two or three hours undisturbed, walking about the room and sitting in an armchair, that restores my equilibrium. It is by turning over things in my mind that the precipitate [an oddly chemical use of the word] is formed out of which the speeches come, and if I don't go through that curious preparatory cud-chewing, then the work suffers' (Robert Rhodes James, *Memoirs of a Conservative*, page 197).

literary illusion and ruminative aphorism. The words had to be carefully chosen so as to be at once simple and evocative. He must not be cleverly cynical like Lloyd George, or abrasive like Birkenhead, or pompous like Curzon or even olympianly cold like Balfour. He must speak from the heart. And there are few effects which require more time or effort to achieve. Even with the devoted and skilful help of Tom Jones, these excursions into literature and the borderlands of philosophy cut heavily into his working days.

It follows almost necessarily from this pattern of life and work that Baldwin's main decisions were taken by highly intuitive methods and often in unorthodox places. He was far from proceeding by relentless ratiocination after the careful assembly and study of all the available evidence upon the Cabinet table. He did not necessarily avoid decisions. On the contrary, in the early part of his leadership at least, he was arguably too precipitous. 'He takes a leap in the dark,' was one of Birkenhead's unfriendly complaints, 'looks round, and takes another.'[4]

In the first autumn of his premiership he not merely took a leap in the dark but decided upon an expedition into the profound obscurity of political outer space. That year he had less time at Aix than usual. He did not leave London until 25 August, and he was back in Paris by 18 September for the only attempt which he ever made, as head of government, to negotiate direct with a foreign statesman. Twenty-four hours of Monsieur Poincaré was more than enough for him. Thereafter he decided that this was a job for Foreign Secretaries. It was left to Neville Chamberlain, fifteen months after Baldwin's retirement, to revive Prime Ministerial diplomacy at Berchtesgaden.

That summer at Aix was not only brief but troubled. The past year, since his previous sojourn at the Hôtel Splendide, had been by far the most spectacular of his life. He had gone home to face crisis and, as he persuaded himself, subsequent obscurity. In fact he had broken the most famous statesman of

Europe, and within six months succeeded to Lloyd George's place if not to his fame. He had already imposed his personality upon the country in a way that Bonar Law in eleven years of intermittent Conservative leadership had never succeeded in doing. But he had not moulded the politics of Britain into a form which he thought he could control. His Cabinet was not his own but an inheritance from Law. The only appointment of significance which he had made himself was that of Neville Chamberlain as Chancellor, and that had been done only two days before the beginning of his holiday. Until then he had, like Law before him, been waiting for McKenna. The hold of that secondary Liberal figure upon successive Conservative leaders is one of the least easily explicable features of the politics of the early 1920s. Baldwin's real need was to reunite the Conservative Party. The Exchequer was the only great plum at his disposal for this purpose. Why he should have dangled it for three months before an undistinguished ex-Chancellor of another party who did not even possess a seat in Parliament defies explanation.

The superficial justification was that he was frightened of the emergence of a centre party, and thought he must try to pre-empt this. But the danger of a centre party came not from McKenna but from the Unionist ex-Coalitionists, led by Austen Chamberlain, who had twice previously been Chancellor, and who, if he was to be brought back into the fold, would clearly require some substantial offer. Instead of the Exchequer, Baldwin had offered him the embassy to Washington, which Chamberlain had rejected with anger. 'The discourtesy shown to me, down to the last detail . . . was not expected and I profoundly resent it,'[5] he wrote to his brother after a visit to the new Prime Minister at Chequers.* It was one of Baldwin's rare failures in human relationships. There were understandable complications. He had been Chamberlain's junior minister,

* Offers of the Washington Embassy, made by Conservative leaders to their predecessors, do not have a happy history. Mr Heath was not pleased by such a proposal from Mrs Thatcher in 1979.

and the rapid reversal of position, combined with Chamberlain's habitual stiffness of manner, probably made his touch less sure than usual. In addition, Chamberlain was not willing to join the Government without Birkenhead, and Birkenhead was strongly disapproved of by the Conservative rank and file, both in the House and in the country, and particularly by those somewhat prim and self-righteous parts of it in which lay Baldwin's greatest strength.

After three months of office Baldwin was not very happy either with his Cabinet or with the state of his party. His pleasure that Curzon had agreed to serve under him had quickly evaporated. He had got the weakest of the Coalitionists, and the one whose health was beginning to fail. In addition Curzon fairly soon reverted to his habit of complaining about the way in which he was treated by his Prime Minister.* Altogether Baldwin, like most Prime Ministers who succeed a member of their own party during a Parliament, felt that he would be happier and stronger if he could make his own Cabinet afresh, and yet was inhibited from so doing.

More importantly, he felt uneasy with the pattern of politics. What Baldwin wanted was a reversion to the firm two-party system of his youth, but with the Labour Party securely established as a great party of state and the Liberal Party tucked up in the history books. He wanted Asquith on a pedestal and Lloyd George in an isolation hospital. He was much clearer in this view than any of his Conservative contemporaries. He had been almost the first to express his belief in the certainty of a

---

* With Lloyd George, of whom he was frightened, he did it behind his back. 'Girlie, I am getting very tired of working or trying to work with that man,' he wrote to his wife in 1921. 'He wants his Forn. Sec. to be a valet almost a drudge and he has no regard for the convenances or civilities of official life.' With Baldwin, of whom he was not frightened, he did it to his face: 'I must confess,' he wrote in the autumn of 1923, 'I am almost in despair as to the way in which foreign policy is carried on in this Cabinet. Any member may make any suggestion he pleases and and the discussion wanders off into hopeless irrelevancies . . . No decision is arrived at and no policy prepared. Do please let us revert to the time-honoured procedure . . . we must act together and the P.M. must see his F.S. through.' It is not clear what was the 'time-honoured procedure' to which Curzon referred with such nostalgia. He had served in no Cabinet before that of Lloyd George.

future Labour Government.* He wanted a reunited Conservative Party, with himself firmly in the saddle, sharing power on a somewhat unequal basis with a Labour Party purged of its extremists by the occasional responsibilities of office. He wanted no instability in the middle.

The two threats to this development which he saw in that late summer of 1923 were Lloyd George and unemployment. Unemployment, which had risen beyond 2 million with the collapse of the post-war boom, had settled back to about 1½ million. This was much higher than pre-war figures, and there seemed little prospect, on existing policies, of any significant decline. Indeed the position of coal, still by far Britain's largest industry, was artificially and temporarily favourable because of the French occupation of the Ruhr.

Baldwin disliked the level of unemployment both for its own sake and because he believed it worked against the evolution of a moderate Labour Party. In common with most of his contemporaries, he comprehended few methods by which governments could affect the total of demand. The best that could be done was to influence its shape in a way that gave the greatest help to the home market. This meant protection. But protection also meant an early election, for Bonar Law had given a pledge a year earlier that there would be no fundamental change in fiscal arrangements without another appeal to the country.

Lloyd George was about to go to America, but Baldwin believed that, on his return in late October, unless pre-empted, he would play the protectionist card. Certainly Lloyd George had never been a doctrinaire free-trader. Nor had he ever allowed such doctrines as had influenced him to sit too heavily upon his shoulders. And if he went protectionist while the Government havered, his attraction for the dissident Conservatives would become still stronger.

Baldwin contemplated all this at Aix, and made up his mind both to go for protection and to put at risk the first independent

* Page 58 *supra*.

Conservative majority for two decades. About the time and place of this extraordinarily bold decision there seems little doubt. Baldwin confirmed it twenty years later, when he wrote to Tom Jones from the depths of his retirement: 'I spent a lot of my holiday in 1923 walking in the hills around Aix and thought it all out by myself. I came to the decision by myself and how I drove that Cabinet to take the plunge I shall never know! I must have more push than people think. . . .'[6]

By itself this statement, unequivocal though it was, could not be regarded as decisive evidence. Even the most honest of men find it surprisingly easy, through the film of time, to recall their own actions quite differently from the way in which objective evidence makes it clear they in fact occurred. And Baldwin in 1943, isolated and unpopular, might well have been tempted, as the tone of his note indeed suggests, to exaggerate his erstwhile capacity for independent decision. But the objective evidence is here on his side. And so is the subjective evidence. He had decided at Aix the year before to break one mould. His decision had been triumphantly vindicated. Now, once more, he found an uncomfortable mould setting around him. It was naturally tempting for a rather superstitious man to trust again to an intuitive judgment of his own made in much the same circumstances as in the previous year.

What is much more difficult to know is what were his motives for the decision, and what he expected to be the likely outcome. Was it the pattern of politics or the future of Britain's trading arrangements which he wished primarily to influence? If the former, then the decision, after a nerve-testing time-lag, was a brilliant success. Within fifteen months he secured a reunited Conservative Party, which gave him the longest uninterrupted party premiership between Asquith and Attlee, the final reduction to a rump of the Liberal Party, and a brief, innocuous baptism of power for the Labour Party. The centre party was dead, Lloyd George was corralled, and the Labour front bench had become a collection of respectable Privy Councillors. It was everything for which he could have asked.

If, on the other hand, it was the freedom to use protection as a weapon against unemployment with which he was primarily concerned, the decision was a disastrous failure. It set back this possibility for nearly a decade, until after the slump had sent unemployment to twice the 'unacceptable' level of 1923 and the pattern of politics had once again been changed.

The difficulty in determining the motive for Baldwin's decision is that he was himself as contradictory about this as he was clear about where and how he took it. In public he put it all on unemployment. In his October speech to the Conservative Party Conference at Plymouth, in which he announced his new position, he said:

> To me, at least, the unemployment problem is the most critical problem of our country. I can fight it. I am willing to fight it. I cannot fight it without weapons. . . . I have come to the conclusion myself that the only way of fighting this subject is by protecting the home market.[7]

No doubt at this stage and in public he could hardly have said anything else. But at the beginning of 1925, he changed the emphasis and told the Constitutional Club that it was a long-meditated move to reunite the Conservative Party. Ten years after that he put the main weight on Lloyd George, and told Tom Jones:

> The Goat was in America. He was on the water when I made the speech and the Liberals did not know what to say. I had information he was going protectionist and I had to get in quick. . . . Dished the Goat, as otherwise he would have got the Party with Austen and F.E. [Birkenhead] and there would have been an end to the Tory Party as we know it.*

In 1943, however, Baldwin again switched back to the economic motive. 'I wanted it', he concluded the note already

---

* This passage, unlike most of Jones's recordings of Baldwin's views, signally fails to catch his rhythm and style. It reads more like a snatch of Attlee's conversation.

quoted, 'because I saw no other weapon then to use in the fight against unemployment.'

Davidson, who was probably the closest of Baldwin's confidents at the time and who also had the advantage of being present at Aix, was equally muddled in his explanations. This may have been because, according to Jones, he attracted most of the blame. In addition he was peculiarly dissatisfied with the outcome of the election, which led to his losing his own, nominally safe, Conservative seat. He put forward the unconvincing view that an election was never part of the plan. Baldwin merely intended to fly a policy kite at Plymouth. Davidson gave the reasons for the kite-flying as partly Lloyd George and partly unemployment.

There is, of course, no reason why Baldwin should have been influenced by one motive to the exclusion of others. It is reasonable, indeed usual, to hope that several consequences will flow from a chosen course of action. But it is desirable to know, in one's own mind at least, what is the primary objective. One disadvantage of intuitive decision-making, or of 'leaps in the dark' if Birkenhead's phraseology is preferred, is that it is not always clear what they are intended to achieve.

The decision once taken, however, Baldwin proceeded to implement it with force and speed. The process illustrated the powers resident in even an untried and hitherto hesitant Prime Minister. There was certain to be a good deal of opposition in the Cabinet. There was indeed something bizarre about the idea that protection was the way to unite the Conservative Party. The issue had been a principal if intermittent source of internal dispute and disruption for the past twenty years. But it ought at least to inspire both the Chamberlains and some others as well.

Baldwin told his Chancellor during the first weekend of October, and then proceeded to consult in ones or twos with other members of the Cabinet, the traditional free traders – Salisbury, Derby, Devonshire and Novar – as well as the natural protectionists – Amery• and Hoare.• He did not meet with much enthusiasm, except from Neville Chamberlain and Amery, but his methods were fairly successful in avoiding the organization of any hostile cabal. The notable exception to his process of consultation was the Foreign Secretary. Curzon did not have any very fixed position on the issue, but he was naturally furious when he discovered the extent of his exclusion. He talked about 'the arbitrary fiat of one weak and ignorant man'. But his influence was in sharp decline, which was no doubt the reason why Baldwin, despite his talk earlier that year about Curzon's 'streak of pure gold', treated him as he did.

The Cabinet did not collectively consider the matter until 22 October, only three days before Baldwin's speech at Plymouth. This, with the path smoothed by prior discussion, had the predictable effect of strengthening the Prime Minister's position. He had to speak. He could not be expected to do so against his own beliefs. The best that could be done was to find a formula which, compatibly with this, gave something to the minority. It took the form of Baldwin agreeing only to speak for himself and of leaving open the question of an election. Concentration upon the working out of this formula had the effect of almost wholly avoiding any serious consideration of the central issue. 'However the discussion happily turned very soon on to the question of procedure,' Amery recorded, 'and the desirability, in which we all concurred, of the statement being so framed as to avoid our being pushed into a general election this autumn.'[8] It was an almost perfect example of how, provided his colleagues have no desire to humiliate him, a Prime Minister can get his way against the better judgment of most of them.

In fact the limitations which Baldwin accepted on this occasion were almost meaningless. Although there is some doubt as to whether or not he appreciated this, he could not commit himself without in practice committing his party – unless he was to be replaced. And as the Conservative Party was already on its third leader within thirteen months, this did not begin to be likely. So far as the avoidance of an election commitment was concerned, this would have been sensible from any point of view. There was no possible reason why he should have wished at that stage to foreclose his options between December and January, or January and the spring. And he could accept the limitation in the knowledge that, when it comes to the point, one of the clearest prerogatives of a Prime Minister is that of choosing the date of an election.

So it proved to be on this occasion. The real restriction of his freedom arose not so much from the restraints of his colleagues as from the fact that his Plymouth speech inevitably created an election atmosphere which he found difficult to control. In the early days of November the members of the Cabinet fell to arguing not whether there should be an election at all upon the issue, but exactly when it should take place. They fell into three groups: at once, January, and April. These groups did not coincide with any previous line-up on the merits of the protectionist issue. The confusion, fortified by a fear on the part of some members that they were going to be asked to make way for Austen Chamberlain and Birkenhead, gave Baldwin almost complete freedom.

On 12 November he decided in favour of an election on 6 December. That afternoon he saw the King, who tried to dissuade him, but, as King George V recorded it: 'He assured me that it was absolutely necessary for him to appeal to the Country as he had gone so far that it was not possible for him to change his mind.'[9] So much for the need of a Prime Minister to obtain the Sovereign's 'permission' for a dissolution of Parliament. The King rather shrewdly asked whether Baldwin had the support of his colleagues in the House of Lords. Baldwin turned the question by saying that 'several of them were, perhaps, too Conservative and did not want a change.' None of them pushed their opposition to the point of resignation, although there was a good deal of muttering and discussion. Negotiations to bring Austen Chamberlain and Birkenhead into the Government broke down.

AN UNSETTLED LEADERSHIP · 77

The King also asked whether the election would not reunite the Liberal Party. 'Yes,' said Baldwin, 'and no bad thing either.' That was not the unity of which he was frightened. Lloyd George had already boxed the compass by declaring himself an 'unrepentant and convinced free trader'; Baldwin's policy, he said, was 'unutterable folly'. He and Asquith even appeared together on the same platform.

Throughout the campaign Baldwin believed he was going to win. So did his party agents. On 4 December, the Conservative Central Office predicted a majority of 87. He set off cheerfully for a final phase in Worcestershire, saying complacently, 'I don't want any bands here when I come back.'[10] There was no danger of embarrassing musical honours. The Government found itself not in a majority of 87 but in a minority of 92. The Conservatives remained the largest party, with 257 seats, but Labour and Liberal combined were 349. The Liberal gains were bigger, but Labour, with 191 seats, remained the second largest party. Baldwin returned to Downing Street as a defeated Prime Minister. The policy which he had put before the country had been decisively rejected. There could be no question of his continuing in office. Almost any other arrangement was possible. There could be a switch to another Conservative Prime Minister, who, uninvolved in the protection *débâcle*, might hope for at any rate some Liberal support. There could be a 'non-party' Government under a venerable statesman of broad appeal: Grey's name was mentioned. There could be an Asquith Government with Conservative support and possibly participation; but this would make a charade of the issue on which the election had been fought. There could be an Asquith Government with Labour support and participation; but this ran directly counter to the whole Labour belief in independence, and would in any event mean the greater opposition party accepting the leadership of the lesser one. Or there could be a straight MacDonald Government, with Liberal support but without Liberal participation.

Of all these possibilities the first was the one which would have been most damaging to Baldwin. It would have meant humiliation, and the end, without much chance of resurrection, of one of the shortest-lived and most disastrous party leaderships in British political history. Baldwin might have precipitated this had he resigned immediately. At first he thought he should. There was a good deal of plotting in the Cabinet, and amongst the dissident ex-Coalitionists. Balfour hovered on the edge of the plot. Then he pronounced himself in favour of Baldwin remaining in office to meet Parliament. This had the advantage of giving a Christmas respite of six weeks. It was perfectly proper constitutionally. There was a confused position and Baldwin was entitled to continue until the oppositions could show that they could and would defeat him in the House of Commons. It also had the advantage of avoiding any suddenness in the Baldwins' departure from Chequers and 10 Downing Street. After a day or two of hesitation, Baldwin decided on this course.

The plot then fell away. There was a good deal of continued muttering, but no real alternative Conservative leader available. In the meantime, opinion began to move towards the last of the possibilities – and the one which suited Baldwin the best – a minority Labour Government. Asquith pronounced that this was the right course, and that was decisive, particularly as Baldwin agreed with him. The great experiment would take place with MacDonald able to count upon less than a third of the members of the House of Commons. He could hardly be more circumscribed. The traditional parties could hardly feel safer.

As these matters became settled, Baldwin's mood became almost euphoric. He went off happily for Christmas in Worcestershire:

> We had snow from London to the Cotswolds and then it turned soft [he wrote to the Davidsons]. Yesterday was a jewel for beauty. Transparently clear, all the country in a deep russet dress, long, vividly bright, horizontal

sunshine casting long shadows in the morning; a dull midday and then a divine evening. I wrote sixty-two letters of thanks. . . . This is a time for hanging out signals to our friends.[11]

As his impending defeat in the House of Commons approached, he became still more cheerful. On the evening when he was to undergo the experience, unique for a Prime Minister of this century, of winding up a debate with the certain knowledge of defeat at the end of his speech, Tom Jones saw him in his room behind the Speaker's chair. 'I have not felt so well for a long time,' he told the ever-comforting Jones, 'and shall be tempted to be very vulgar in my speech.'[12] His 'vulgarity' did not extend much further than a quotation from Dryden, but he spoke with gusto and good humour. The Government went down by 71 votes and after a short Cabinet on the next morning (22 January 1924) he drove to Buckingham Palace and resigned. MacDonald took office the same afternoon.

Baldwin had two immediate tasks to perform in opposition. He had to make it clear that he had learnt his lesson on tariff reform, and to do this in a way as compatible as possible with the dignity of an ex-Prime Minister. Derby, with the support of Salvidge,* his Liverpool henchman, was making this difficult by trying to conduct a growling inquest into the whole election strategy. Baldwin lanced this boil fairly quickly and quietly by an announcement to a party meeting on 11 February: 'I do not feel justified in advising the party again to submit the proposal for a general tariff to the country except on the clear evidence that on this matter public opinion is disposed to reconsider its judgment of two months ago.' It was a little circumlocutory, but it is never wise for a politican to use ringing words to announce a retreat.

His second task was to bring Austen Chamberlain back into

* Sir Archibald Salvidge (1863–1928) was principal Conservative Party organizer in Liverpool; an extremely effective mobilizer, with some brewery assistance, of the working class Protestant Tory vote; and partly because of a special relationship with Derby, probably the most nationally influential local agent of any party during this century.

full communion. This was easier in opposition than in government. No policy orthodoxy had to be imposed and no places had to be found for clients of the former leader who wished to be junior ministers. There was only the perennial problem of Birkenhead. 'If Birkenhead stood alone,' Baldwin self-righteously pronounced, 'I would not touch him with a barge-pole.'[13] But Birkenhead did not stand alone. Austen Chamberlain, despite his limitations, was an ally of a staunchness rarely seen in politics. Baldwin had a reconciliation dinner with Austen at Neville Chamberlain's house on 4 February. He made an offer to Austen, and authorized him to convey one to Birkenhead. Both were accepted. Sir Robert Horne also joined the Shadow Cabinet. 'So reunion has come at last, thanks, I think I may say, to me,' Neville Chamberlain wrote to his sister.[14]

Thanks to whoever it was, Baldwin by the spring of 1924 was making surprisingly good progress toward the political objectives which he had set himself the previous autumn. His morale was moderately high, but no more. He had private troubles, associated both with his eldest son and with a shortage of money. Baldwins Ltd had paid no dividend for several years running. His income was less than a half of what it had been before 1914, and he was losing capital too. The value of the firm's shares, which had been 50/- when he made his generous 'F.S.T.' gesture, fell steadily from 1920 onwards until they reached 3/6 in 1927 and then went down to 1/8 in 1931. Of course he had some other assets, but the collapse of the central part of his fortune did not make for buoyancy.

Nor did he enjoy the business of parliamentary opposition. His *forte* as Prime Minister was taking the heat out of debates and convincing the House of the reasonableness of the Government's approach. It was a technique which by its very nature was unsuited for use from the front opposition bench. He recognized his limitations, but he made little attempt to develop another technique. He was a gentle opponent to a weak Government.

Both his attitude and his easy pattern of life is well-illustrated by Tom Jones's account of a morning in April that year. Jones was in his room in the Cabinet Offices, carrying on the routine business of a Labour Government, of which paradoxically he was throughout his life a consistent voting supporter, but enjoying none of the intimacy with MacDonald which he had achieved with each of the three preceding Prime Ministers.

> I was in the middle of papers [he wrote] when Mr Stanley Baldwin was announced at the door. I was startled for a moment, as one does not have ex-Prime Ministers calling on one every day, but this was very like S.B., who began, 'You will never come to see me, so I thought I would come to see you.' We gossiped for half an hour in the office and then walked up to the United Universities Club and had lunch. After asking how I was getting on he told me something of the worries of a Party leader in days when there are no deep political convictions to divide men of good will. He had some troublesome followers who were clamouring for a positive policy without being able to suggest one. The one he had offered had been rejected. There was nothing for it but to await events. . . . He joked about having to go on making speeches without my help. . . .[15]

Outside the House Baldwin forced the pace a little more. In May and June he made an important and successful series of speeches throughout the country, laying down a social reform policy for a future Conservative Government. The effect of these was temporarily marred by an interview of quite startling indiscretion which he gave to the *People* newspaper, then very right-wing and hardly distinguished. It was a surprising vehicle for Baldwin to choose. Probably the Conservative Central Office had arranged it. He saw an unknown reporter alone and did not check the copy. As a result the paper came out with the most terrifying remarks allegedly made by Baldwin about some of the political figures of the day, notably Beaverbrook, but also Lloyd George and others. Denials had to be issued, if only to reduce the risk of libel. The further trouble was that the 'unknown' journalist had caught Baldwin's method of expression, and indeed his private views, almost perfectly. Few were much convinced by the denials, and the proprietor, editor and staff of the *People* were quite naturally furious at this behaviour on the part of 'Honest Stanley'. It left a little dent in his reputation, but like most such incidents, was a quickly subsiding storm in a teacup.

All things considered, he departed for Aix in that summer of 1924 in calmer mind than in either of the two previous years. The Labour Government's hold on office was manifestly tenuous. A third quick election was clearly a possibility. His chances of winning it with a reunited party and a substantial majority were good. So long as he did so, his leadership was not under challenge.

Parliament reassembled after only a seven-week recess on 30 September. The future of the Government was at risk over the ratification of treaties with the Soviet Union. In the event it was heavily defeated on 8 October on the issue of the Campbell Case*. The campaign was disfigured by Conservative exploitation of the forged Zinoviev letter† and of the Bolshevik issue

---

* J. R. Campbell (1894–1969), holder of the Military Medal for gallantry in the First World War and much later editor of the *Daily Worker*, was at that time temporarily acting as editor of the *Workers' Weekly*. As a result of an article urging soldiers to let it be known that neither in the class war nor in a military war should they turn their guns upon their fellow workers, the Director of Public Prosecutions recommended that he be prosecuted for sedition. The Attorney-General (Sir Patrick Hastings) concurred and Campbell was arrested. This led to a storm on the left of the Labour Party. Hastings consulted the Cabinet and withdrew the prosecution, claiming that he reached the decision on his own and not as a result of the Cabinet discussion. This led to a slowly mounting storm on the right, culminating in a major debate on 8 October, a Conservative censure motion and a Liberal amendment to refer the matter to a Select Committee. MacDonald resisted both. At the end the Conservatives voted for the Liberal amendment to their own motion and the Government was defeated by 364 to 198. MacDonald asked for and was granted an immediate dissolution, which nobody greatly wanted as it was the third within twenty-four months.

† A letter purporting to be from Grigori Zinoviev, the President of the Communist International, to the British Communist Party giving them instructions for military infiltration and other measures 'to develop the ideas of Leninism in England'. It started life in the offices of the *Daily Mail* but was widely accepted as authentic by other

generally. Baldwin soiled his hands a little, but not excessively. His general note was one of chiding MacDonald for the weakness of his control over his own extremists and suggesting that what the country needed was men of practical experience, breadth of view and lack of dogmatic commitment.

His most effective performance – except that there were not at that stage a great many people who were able to listen – was his broadcast. No one really knew how the new technique should be handled. MacDonald decided, naturally but disastrously, that the obvious objective was to import into the living rooms of the wireless-owning population the soaring platform oratory which so moved his immediate audiences. The BBC broadcast him live from a mass meeting in Glasgow. He sounded ranting and inconsequential. Baldwin by contrast spoke intimately from the office of the Director-General. The result was a triumph. He had found a method of neutralising MacDonald's most effective political quality – his inspirational personal presence.

The result of the election was also a triumph. The Conservatives increased their vote by the sensational proportion of 37 per cent. They won 419 seats, against 151 for Labour and 40 (a loss of 116) for the Liberals. Almost the only place where the Conservatives did badly was the normally impregnable Birmingham. This hardly diminished Baldwin's sense of personal victory. He had been unopposed at Bewdley, but his two principal colleagues, the Chamberlain brothers, found their majorities uncomfortably reduced, Neville's to the very edge of defeat.

The virtual destruction of the Liberal Party almost completed the political pattern which he had hoped for since the previous autumn. '. . . I did not think it would come so quickly,' he told Tom Jones on 4 November. 'The next step must be the elimination of the Communists by Labour. Then we shall have two

---

newspapers, by the Foreign Office and indeed by MacDonald, who was Foreign Secretary as well as Prime Minister. Trying to deal with the matter in the interstices of a punishing speaking tour, MacDonald handled it with great maladroitness.

parties, the party of the Right, and the party of the Left.'[16] He had just been to the Palace to kiss hands as Prime Minister for the second time.

He turned to Cabinet-making. His position was quite different from that of 1923. He had won his own victory. He had the prospect of four years or so of uninterrupted power. He could build his own Government with few debts or commitments. And he had at his disposal almost an embarrassment rather than a shortage of political experience. He approached his task, as Austen Chamberlain noted, with a new firmness and confidence. But on the whole he discharged it badly.

He started well by making it clear to a shocked and protesting Curzon that he could not again be Foreign Secretary. In his place he put Austen Chamberlain, although a little more by accident than design, for Baldwin had offered him the choice between that and the India Office. When Chamberlain chose the senior office, Birkenhead got India.

The domestic appointments were more eccentric. Neville Chamberlain was naturally offered a return to the Treasury. With a lack of concern for place which was worthy of his father, he said he would rather be Minister of Health.* Baldwin then inclined to Sir Samuel Hoare for the Chancellorship. Neville Chamberlain suggested Churchill. It was an extraordinary suggestion to come from a man who was normally so sensitive to Conservative Party opinion. Churchill had only recently rejoined the party. Eight months before he had fought as an independent against an official Conservative at a bye-election in the Abbey division of Westminster. Moreover he knew nothing about finance, and had no discernible claim to so senior an appointment. What was equally extraordinary was that Baldwin jumped at the idea. Ten minutes later – another leap in the dark – he offered the appointment to Churchill. Churchill, who at first thought it was the Chancellorship of the

---

* The Ministry of Health had thirty years of somewhat misnamed life, beginning in 1919. Its responsibilities covered local government, housing and all social welfare schemes.

Duchy of Lancaster which was the proposition and for which he would happily have settled, accepted the greater post with tears in his eyes and an expression of grateful loyalty. 'You have done more for me than Lloyd George ever did,' he said.[17] So, indeed, Baldwin had. He had also paid a substantial price for the pleasure, not merely of looking at the corpse of the idea of a centre party, but of stamping upon it several times over.

He made Joynson-Hicks* (good on penal reform but illiberal on all else) Home Secretary, and thus firmly launched the Home Office, which had been different in the days of Harcourt, Asquith and Churchill, upon a course of dour obscurantism from which it took three or four decades to recover. His worst mistake was at the Ministry of Labour, which, foreseeably, turned out to be the crucial sector of his Government's battlefront. He appointed Steel-Maitland,* another ten-minute decision, after Horne had refused, despite the fact that he told Tom Jones he had spent eighteen months contemplating the importance of the post: 'Neville recommended S-M. He is able enough – got all those Firsts at Oxford – but is he human enough? . . . He will do well administering the Office, but I am frankly afraid of him in the House.' The outcome (perhaps this would have happened whoever had been at the Ministry of Labour) was that most of the principal figures of the Government devoted a good part of their time to assisting Steel-Maitland in his job.

Baldwin's other error was not to include Balfour. That magnificent old cat of British politics was seventy-six. But as he was brought in six months later when Curzon died, age was hardly a reason for excluding him from an office without portfolio in 1924. Hankey,* the Secretary of the Cabinet, thought it was because he gave Baldwin 'a certain sense of *gaucherie* and inferiority'.[18]

So Balfour did to many people. But Baldwin had less occasion to feel it than most. He may have constructed his Cabinet a little amiss, but he had constructed his power-base superbly. After an uneasy eighteen months he was in a stronger position than any Conservative leader since Lord Salisbury.

CHAPTER FOUR

The Perplexity of Power

Baldwin's second premiership lasted four and a half years. It was the second longest period of party power, uninterrupted by either an election or a change of leadership, of this century.* It was also a government of great stability of men in offices. Baldwin was perhaps the last Prime Minister to treat his Cabinet colleagues, as Gladstone had done, as members of a college of cardinals. Once nominated, he had to live with them. He would no more have thought of behaving as Harold Macmillan did in 1962, and dismissing nearly a half of them as though they were junior executives in an ailing company, than it would have occurred to him to divorce his wife and marry one of his walking companions. Nor did he shuffle them around, as an almost annual political gymkhana, in the way that Harold Wilson did. Once a minister in the main Baldwin Government, you were there, and in the same office, for the duration. Only death or impending death (Curzon and Cave), acute shortage of money and the need to seek the sustenance of the City (Birkenhead), a policy resignation (Cecil of Chelwood•), or appointment as Viceroy of India (Edward Wood, later Lord Irwin, later Lord Halifax•) produced changes. For the rest, the only variety was provided by the decision of the President of the Board of Trade, somewhat eccentrically as it now appears, to change his name from Lloyd-Greame to Cunliffe-Lister.†

* The first parliament of the Attlee Government, from July 1945 to February 1950, was the longest.
† There was of course money involved. He changed it again in 1935 to Lord Swinton. He was made an earl twenty years after that but, surprisingly, missed the opportunity for a third change. Born in 1884, he lived until 1972.

This did not mean that there were no undulations in Baldwin's relations with his Cabinet. With the exception of Bridgeman,• the First Lord of the Admiralty, it is doubtful whether he was on close personal terms with any of them. Neville Chamberlain, the Minister of Health, would probably, and with justice, have been his choice as the most efficient minister. There was a close working partnership between them, in governments and in opposition, for fifteen years, but it was untinted by much mutual affection or even comprehension. Chamberlain was constantly irritated by Baldwin's whimsical and indolent manner.* He forgave it only because of his party loyalty and his equally constant recognition, honest, reluctant, surprised, of the value to the Conservative Party of Baldwin's unique position in the country.

The Cabinet member of whom Baldwin's opinion rose most rapidly was Birkenhead. He trusted him on India, but also used him on the most sensitive domestic issues. When Birkenhead left office in 1928, Baldwin accepted his resignation with a reluctance which was convincing because honestly expressed: 'We shall part, on my side at least, with a feeling of personal regret which I could not have believed possible four years ago.'[1] Birkenhead, who had written after the victory of 1924 of 'the tragedy that so great an Army should have so uninspiring a Commander in Chief' and was usually more sparing with his admiration than with his criticism, allowed some balancing increase of his own regard for Baldwin to occur. But it stopped well short of friendship. He would hardly have been a natural companion for the Prime Minister, Mrs Baldwin and Tom

---

* This is exemplified (although not much to Chamberlain's credit) by a 1925 incident. 'I had noticed,' Chamberlain wrote in his diary after a Cabinet at which he had been expounding a departmental problem, 'that S.B. didn't seem to be attending to me, and presently he passed an open note across the table to Winston, who was sitting beside me. On the note was written:
MATCHES
Lent at 10.30 a.m.
Returned?
This triviality, while a very grave question was being discussed under S.B.'s chairmanship, made the most deplorable impression on me' (David Dilks, *Neville Chamberlain*, vol. 1 1869–1929, pages 448–9).

Jones during a quiet evening of patience in the Long Gallery at Chequers.

The same was substantially true of Churchill. But he and the Prime Minister saw each other frequently, although rarely on social occasions. The Chancellor's headquarters were then Queen Anne's Throne Room in what is now the Cabinet Office, and the nearest route to it from 11 Downing Street lay through the connecting doors of number 10. It became the Chancellor's habit to interrupt his morning procession to work for a few minutes of Cabinet Room conversation with the Prime Minister. It was a habit which helped to avoid any major personal quarrels between them until after the demise of the Government. This was despite the fact that Churchill, amazingly for a new and over-rewarded recruit to the Conservative Party who twelve years before had nearly broken up the Asquith Cabinet with his demand for a larger navy, began his Chancellorship by presenting an importunate demand to the Admiralty ministers (who were Baldwin's closest friends in the Government – Davidson was the junior minister) for a slashing of the cruiser replacement programme. A major Cabinet dispute rumbled on for nearly a year. Resignations, both of ministers and of admirals but not of the Chancellor, were threatened. Eventually there was a settlement which leant in the Admiralty direction. Churchill had shown himself as kaleidoscopic as he was departmentally combative. He brought with him into the Treasury few old prejudices beyond the self-confidence of his conviction that whatever he believed in at a particular time was right.

The two most senior members of the Government were Balfour (who joined as Lord President after Curzon's death) and Austen Chamberlain. Both had been leaders of the Conservative Party. With neither did Baldwin establish very easy relations. Balfour's charm was too subtle and serpentine for him. And with Austen Chamberlain there was always the old difficulty of a stiff man who had once been so much his senior. Baldwin gave him his head as Foreign Secretary and supported him well. It required the full backing of the Prime Minister to get the Locarno Treaty through the Cabinet. But no intimacy was ever established. This was more for personal reasons than because of Baldwin's alleged lack of interest in foreign affairs. He ran them, admittedly, on a loose rein. He devoted very little of his time to seeing foreigners. He hardly talked to any, except for the waiters in the hotel at Aix-les-Bains. He was also full of the widespread English anti-American prejudice of the 1920s, and he found French diplomatic life a little too rich, both politically and gastronomically, for his stomach. He never made the seventy-mile journey from Aix to Geneva, which was then the centre of the international world. It was rather as though Attlee or Macmillan had spent post-war autumn holidays at Saratoga Springs while eschewing any contact with the United Nations in New York. But Baldwin would move to see Austen Chamberlain, provided it was not to Geneva. 'Whatever you do, I will support you,' he wrote in 1927, 'and if you want to have a talk I will meet you at Annecy at lunch any day you care to name. . . .'[2]

Yet, such were the curious contradictions of his character that Baldwin always remained closely in touch with the work of the Foreign Office. Austen Chamberlain, the second man in the Government, went rarely to Chequers and never to Astley. Sir William Tyrrell,• one of the less distinguished of the chain of Foreign Office permanent under-secretaries, stayed at Chequers almost once a month, and occasionally at Astley. With a more interfering Prime Minister and a more suspicious Foreign Secretary it would not have been a happy arrangement.

By the end of his Government Baldwin was anxious to make a whole series of Cabinet changes. A number of ministers, including Austen Chamberlain, were manifestly tired or worse. Baldwin contemplated the happy idea of asking everyone who was older than himself to go. This would remove Balfour, Salisbury, Joynson-Hicks, Cushendun• and Bridgeman, but also Austen Chamberlain, of whom he felt he could not dispose. Churchill had been long enough at the Treasury, and could perhaps go to the India Office. Neville Chamberlain must clearly be persuaded to accept promotion and another, longer, spell at the Treasury. Steel-Maitland could at last be moved from the Ministry of Labour, which had in many ways been the key departmental post of the administration, and in which he had throughout been ill-regarded but undisturbed. But perhaps the changes were better postponed until after the election. The country might prefer a tired to an unfamiliar team. So, at any rate, Baldwin decided. The election came first and the changes were never made.

Baldwin's practice of dedicated delegation was not confined to foreign affairs. The great events of his administration were the return to the gold standard, the Treaty of Locarno, the General Strike, the Imperial Conference of 1926 which led on to the Statute of Westminster, and the measures originating in the Ministry of Health for the reform of local government and the extension of social security.

With only one of these five major developments was Baldwin centrally concerned. The return to gold was Churchill's decision, even though, within the Treasury, he at first was hard to convince. Baldwin then made no demur against the Chancellor's recommendation; there would have been a greater chance of his demurring had the decision gone the other way, not because of his views but because of his admiration and affection for Montagu Norman, the intellectually certain Governor of the Bank of England.

Locarno was primarily Austen Chamberlain's work, and the Ministry of Health reforms perhaps even more decisively that of Neville Chamberlain. The elegant formula which enabled the dignity of the Crown to be combined with the reality of Dominion independence came from Balfour. Only in the case of the General Strike and the events which surrounded it did the participation of the Prime Minister match his degree of ultimate responsibility. His full involvement here was as inevitable as it was appropriate. Industrial relations, as the subject today would be described, was an area in which he instinctively felt himself at home. The combination of his gentle business experience, his belief in the politics of personal relationships and his patience in waiting for a desired outcome were unusual and valuable qualities. They were admirably suited to a problem of framework or atmosphere. But that was by no means the core of his problem. This was the harder, more practical issue of the future of the coal industry. It employed over a million men. Its product was of overwhelming importance to the fuel needs of the nation. It was also geared, particularly in certain districts, to a large export trade. For this trade the industry had failed to maintain its pre-war competitiveness. There had been big profits before and during the war, but little investment or improvement of method. The collieries were run by one of the most obscurantist bodies of employers in the country, known collectively and appropriately as 'the owners'. They had built up the industry on cheap labour, and their only answer to the challenge of foreign competition was to attempt to cut back the limited improvements in wages and hours which had been secured during and immediately after the war.

They were confronted by mining communities which were close-knit, isolated, well-organized, and intensely internally loyal. Only in the Midlands, where the methods were more modern and the communities less separate, was there some doubt about the solidarity of the miners. Elsewhere, in South Wales, in Durham, in Yorkshire, in Scotland, they were the best-trained, most battle-scarred fighting troops of organized labour. As a huge union they were powerful in the Trades Union Congress. Many of the most influential other union leaders, Thomas• from the right wing, Bevin from the left-centre (which was his position in those days), might have considerable doubt about the tactical skill of the miners' leaders. But they had no doubt about the emotional hold of the miners over the Labour movement. The miners occupied the central sector of the industrial battlefront. Baldwin's task, if he wanted peace, was to prevent this sector from flaring into conflict. If he wanted victory, it was to separate the miners from their half-reluctant allies.

Which did he want? The answer, as was often the case with Baldwin, was that he did not quite know. But this indeterminedness was neither unique nor wholly surprising. He wanted, from his own point of view, as much as he could get of the best of both worlds. He wanted peace, provided it was compatible with the superiority of the state and the then accepted view of that somewhat shifting concept, the sanctity of private property. If peace was not obtainable on these terms, then of course he wanted victory, and he wanted to know before he started the battle that he could be certain of gaining it. But he also wanted the battle to be as bloodless as possible. He knew he would have to live afterwards with the vanquished. He did not wish to make a desert and call it peace. What he did wish was to emasculate his opponents, and then to pretend they were coming together as equals.

Where he was intellectually confused was that he failed to see any close connection between the economic stance of his Government and its industrial problems. He once shone a surprising shaft of original light on to the economic scene. In 1924 he spoke in the House of Commons of the need to reduce exports. The general view was that this was a slip of the tongue for 'imports', but Baldwin when questioned persisted in his first statement. What he meant was that, with the terms of trade running strongly in Britain's favour and with a substantial underuse of resources, the economy was too much directed towards the depressed export trades – coal, steel, shipbuilding and cotton – and not enough towards newer industries which would mainly supply an enlarged home market. It was a fumbling towards the shift of men and activity from South Wales to the Slough Trading Estate or from Scotland to the Ford factory at Dagenham which symbolized the economic geography of the later period of his power. But it was one thing to want to see some medium-term alteration of the shape of

British industry. It was another – particularly if you were supposedly seeking industrial peace with a full recognition of the crucial position of coal – to pursue an exchange-rate policy which would be certain to make as difficult as possible the transition period for this and other traditional export trades. Yet this is precisely what Baldwin did.

Despite this basic contradiction, he began with a notable act of conciliation. Most Conservative opinion had long been opposed to the system whereby a trade union could contribute to the Labour Party a proportion of each member's subscription, unless the member specially contracted out. They wished to change the rules and require the politically committed members to contract in. For obvious reasons the difference in practice would be substantial. A private member's bill to effect this change was brought forward in late February, 1925. Although there was some division of Conservative opinion, it appeared that a majority both of the Cabinet and of the backbenchers favoured either the acceptance of the bill or a Government measure doing roughly the same job in its place.

Baldwin treated the matter with the utmost seriousness. He made a lot of soundings, appointed a special Cabinet committee to go into the subject, and held a special Cabinet to receive its report. At the special Cabinet, and curiously for a Prime Minister who wishes to get his own way when his colleagues are at best perplexed, he invited everyone else to give their own views before himself intervening. He then delivered what was certainly his most effective Cabinet intervention until that date, and probably his most effective ever. Birkenhead, the chairman of the committee, which had produced rather limp conclusions, is reported to have broken an awed silence to announce that if the Prime Minister spoke to the House as he had just spoken to the Cabinet he would do so with unanimous support and triumphant outcome. Austen Chamberlain was equally enthusiastic at the time, but later put the occasion into somewhat more critical perspective by saying that it was the only time in fourteen years that he had ever known Baldwin to influence a Cabinet decision.*

Baldwin's speech to the House came a week later on a Friday morning. It was the normal time for a private member's bill, but it was certainly not the normal time for a major Prime Ministerial oration. However, he had no difficulty in securing a large and attentive House. His speech lasted about an hour. It was quiet, reminiscent, a little sententious. Its two most memorable passages were, first, a somewhat rose-tinted picture of industrial life in the heyday of his family company ('It was a place where nobody ever got the sack and where . . . a number of old gentlemen used to spend their days sitting on the handles of wheelbarrows smoking their pipes. Oddly enough, it was not an inefficient community'); and, second, a small peace-offering not so much across the floor of the House as across the gulf of industry:

> I want my party today to make a gesture to the country. . . . We have our majority. We believe in the justice of the bill. . . . But we are going to withdraw our hand. We are not going to push our political advantage home at a moment like this. . . . We, at any rate, are not going to fire the first shot. We stand for peace. We stand for the removal of suspicion in the country. We want to create a new atmosphere, a new atmosphere in a new Parliament for a new age, in which the people can come together. . . . We abandon what we have laid our hands to. We know we may be called cowards for doing it. . . . But we believe we know what at this moment the country wants, and we believe it is for us in our strength to do what no other party can do at this moment and to say that we at any rate stand for peace. . . . I have con-

---

* This, as stated, was certainly unfair. Apart from anything else, Chamberlain served with Baldwin for only a little more than a third of the period. It could be the only occasion on which Baldwin *imposed* a policy of his own upon the Cabinet, but there were many other occasions, including some of considerable importance to Chamberlain's conduct of the Foreign Office, when he steered skilfully towards one course rather than another.

fidence in my fellow-countrymen throughout the whole
of Great Britain. Although I know there are those who
work for different ends from most of us in this House,
yet there are many in all ranks and all parties who will
re-echo my prayer: 'Give peace in our time, O Lord.'[3]

The speech killed the bill. It gave Baldwin a position of
exceptional strength. His colleagues nearly all wrote letters of
glowing congratulation. The press was equally warm. The
general verdict was that he had secured his leadership for years
to come. The Labour Party was emotionally confused. Haldane
wrote that he had 'lifted public affairs to a higher level'. A less
judicial member of the Party came up to him in the lobby only
half-convinced, but with tears of emotion running down his
cheeks. Another,* not without judgment or character, wrote
nearly fifteen years later, when Baldwin's reputation was at its
lowest, to compare the speech with the Gettysburg oration.

It was all a little hyperbolic, but it did mean that when, four
months later, the issue shifted from the soft abstractions of
industrial good will in general to the hard reality of reducing
wages in the coal industry, the Prime Minister started with a
store of self-confidence. The miners, having refused to accept
new agreements with reduced wages, were threatened with a
lock-out from 31 July. The TUC, and particularly the other
members of the Triple Alliance,† offered them full support.
'Black Friday' of 1921, when the alliance collapsed in weakness
and recrimination, might be revenged. The prospect of an
imminent General Strike seemed real. An intensive period of
negotiation began. First Bridgeman (both personally and as
First Lord of the Admiralty a very surprising choice), and then

* David Kirkwood (1872–1955), MP for Dumbarton Burghs (1922–51). A
Clydeside firebrand in his early days, a peer in 1951.

† The Triple Alliance, between the miners, the railwaymen and the transport
workers, had been formed in 1919 and secured some partial success in October 1920
when a threatened rail strike in support of the miners produced a compromise wage
offer from Lloyd George. In April 1921, in the second stage of this continuing dispute
the Alliance collapsed, not so much in betrayal (although it was so portrayed by many)
as in confusion. In the mythology of the Labour movement, Friday, 15 April became
'Black Friday'.

Baldwin himself were brought in to sustain Steel-Maitland. But the negotiations were not in Downing Street. Baldwin would go to the Ministry of Labour and there meet both the unions and the owners. Eventually he decided on a temporary surrender. The Government would pay to maintain the *status quo* for nine months. The industry received a subsidy, optimistically calculated at £10 million, but in fact costing £23 million, to keep wages and profits at their existing level. The Prime Minister, very peripatetic in this crisis, went through to 11 Downing Street at 9 o'clock one morning to persuade the Chancellor that it was necessary. He did not have great difficulty with Churchill. He had much more with the press, and somewhat more with the House of Commons. But there was no significant Conservative revolt. Most backbenchers probably appreciated the force of the argument which at that stage had to remain unspoken '. . . we were not ready [for a General Strike],' he subsequently told G. M. Young.[4] Somewhat less laconically, he wrote to the Viceroy in 1927: 'I still think we were right in buying off the strike in 1925, though it proved once more the cost of teaching democracy. Democracy has arrived at a gallop in England and I fear all the time it is a race for life. Can we educate them before the crash comes?'[5]

Part of the arrangement was that there should be an inquiry into the coal industry during the nine months. After discussion of several other names, Sir Herbert Samuel,• Asquith's last Home Secretary, was asked to undertake it. This arranged, the Prime Minister went off to Aix. He returned on 16 September, telling Tom Jones that he now knew what Roosevelt meant when he said he felt like a 'bull moose'.* It was his best holiday since before 1914. He read no papers beyond glancing at *The*

---

* The Roosevelt surname alone still meant Theodore rather than Franklin. Ex-President Theodore Roosevelt had used the phrase at the 1912 Republican Convention in Chicago when he announced that he was running against President Taft, his own choice as his successor in 1908, either on or against the Republican ticket. 'Until then', a chronicler of that conflict wrote, 'a bull moose had simply been the huge-antlered male member of the largest deer family, of the genus *Alces Americana* but TR's simile made it the symbol of a fighting cause' (William Manners, *TR and Will*, pages 237–8). In

Times headlines. If he could keep his physical vigour through the session he 'might get something done'.[6]

The main thing he got done was to defeat the General Strike. Whether it was his intention to provoke the battle it is almost impossible to decide. Certainly the Government used the nine months of respite to ensure that there was no question of again being unready. Careful plans were laid for an effective national strike-breaking organization. This was no more than common prudence. Baldwin could not retreat again on the subsidy, and the prospect of finding a solution without it was dismal.

The Samuel Commission reported on 11 March. It proposed longer-term measures for the reorganization of the industry, including the nationalization of mining royalties, amalgamations and some closures, Government aid for research and improved marketing, and a gradual extension of welfare services into family allowances, holidays, improved housing and some degree of profit-sharing, which were anathema to the owners and unwelcome to the Government. It rejected, in somewhat scathing terms, the owners' proposals for a combination of longer hours and lower wages. Longer hours, indeed, would merely mean more unsold coal. But the report was adamant that, with the retention of the seven-hour day, wages must immediately come down.

After some hesitation the Government announced that they would reluctantly accept the report. Then, during late March and April, they made rather half-hearted and dilatory attempts to get agreement on this basis. Steel-Maitland, Birkenhead and Baldwin himself were the principal intermediaries. The strength of their position, which they did not sufficiently exploit, was that the majority of the TUC, upon whose support the miners depended, preferred the report to a General Strike. The weakness, then and subsequently, was that Baldwin and

---

the event, Roosevelt ran against the Republican ticket, as the champion of the Progressive or 'Bull Moose' Party, and put Woodrow Wilson in the White House by default. I think that Baldwin merely wished to say that he felt very well, and not to arouse these memories.

the others did not really believe in the report. Baldwin was cautious about the longer-term measures, and was constantly attracted by a lengthening of hours in order to assuage the sharpness of the wages conflict.

The miners' leaders were not easy to deal with. A. J. Cook,• the dedicated firebrand from South Wales, and Herbert Smith,• a dour, uncompromising and sometimes uncomprehending Yorkshireman, made a difficult pair. The TUC found them nearly as awkward as did the Government. But their determination was representative and not merely personal. Nor were they always as intransigent as was implied by Cook's famous slogan 'Not a penny off the pay, not a minute on the day'. There was a psychological moment when they might have accepted the report. But Baldwin let it pass. He was too attracted by postponing difficult decisions and too unwilling to coerce the owners. He also made the mistake of trying to frighten the miners with the consequence of sticking to existing conditions. Did Mr Smith appreciate that this might mean 200,000 or more miners being thrown out of work? Yes, Mr Smith did, and he was prepared to face this rather than accept a worsening of conditions. In any event, the shrinkage of the industry was already taking place.

On Friday 23 April Baldwin saw a small delegation of the owners. Tom Jones, devoted though he was to Baldwin, made a revealing comment on the meeting:

> It is impossible not to feel the contrast between the reception which Ministers give to a body of owners and a body of miners. Ministers are at ease with the former, they are friends exploring a situation. There was hardly any indication of opposition or censure. It was rather a joint discussion of whether it was better to precipitate a strike or the unemployment which would result from continuing the present terms. The majority clearly wanted a strike. . . . The P.M. said very little throughout beyond posing an occasional question. He smoked

all the time and at the end asked me to walk with him in the Park. I told him that I thought he was much too gentle in his handling of the miners and the owners, and especially the latter, and that there were a lot of things he ought to have said.[7]

The next day, Baldwin, having shocked Hankey by insisting on retiring to Chequers for the weekend, again sought the solace of Jones's chiding but comforting company. He was summoned down on the Saturday evening and his presence at least had the effect of giving us a vignette of Baldwin's behaviour on the eve of what was likely to be the most testing week of his premiership. When Jones arrived, about seven, he found the Prime Minister reading a novel. Baldwin at once began to talk about the walk they would have the following morning, and suggested that they should eschew the subject of coal for the evening. He failed to live up to this amiable recipe, however, and there was considerable discussion of the issue, discursive rather than purposeful, before dinner. Dinner was a family party of six. As soon as it was over Baldwin went to his wife's room and sat and talked with her until an early bed. Next morning, after a 9.15 breakfast, he discussed with Jones his ideas for a speech he had to make in a few weeks' time at a Literary Fund dinner. At eleven they set off on the heralded and substantial walk. In the course of it there was serious coal discussion. Jones tried to put before him the possible alternative courses of action. Then he suggested that they might get Arthur Pugh,• the moderate leader of the steelworkers who was that year's chairman of the TUC, to come down to Chequers for tea and an exploratory talk. The Prime Minister changed the subject for a few minutes and then agreed.

Before lunch Jones made the necessary arrangements and they both glanced at the Sunday newspapers, apparently for the first time. After lunch Baldwin retreated to his room. Pugh arrived with Sir Horace Wilson,• the permanent secretary of the Ministry of Labour. Baldwin showed them some of the curiosities of the house and gave them tea in the Long Gallery, which he described with more pride than accuracy as 'the finest room in England'. Then he took them to his study for a more serious talk. After an hour Jones and Wilson disappeared and he stayed alone with Pugh and glasses of whisky. Later he pronounced the talk 'invaluable' and retired to Mrs Baldwin's room for a pre-dinner chat. After dinner he played patience and made it clear that 'he had had enough of coal for the day'.[8]

On the Monday morning there was breakfast at 7.45 before departure for London, with no newspapers but with Baldwin full of familiar gossip about his favourite subject, the (Lloyd George) Coalition Government.

> We motored to Wendover. He booked his own tickets. . . . L.G. would have left such a detail to a secretary but S.B. likes to write his own cheques and address his own envelopes. The P.M. bought *The Times*, the *Daily Telegraph*, the *Morning Post*, and a picture paper for Mrs Baldwin. I suggested he should, with a coal crisis on, have bought the *Daily Herald*, which I did. We had a reserved compartment. He read the leading articles in less than five minutes, noticed the news of a friend's death, and then settled down to solve a cross-word puzzle in the *Daily Telegraph*, which he finished just as we steamed into Baker Street.[9]

That day he had three crucial meetings, one with the miners in the morning, a second with the owners in the early evening, and a third with the TUC after dinner. He did not accomplish much, beyond making it clear to the owners that, in return for their agreement to a national minimum, he would abandon Samuel and give them the eight-hour day; but he was thought to have acquitted himself well.

There was a continuing round of meetings, but no serious approach to a formula of settlement until late on the following Saturday night. Baldwin, accompanied by Birkenhead and Steel-Maitland, then met four representatives of the TUC at 11 p.m. By 1.15 a loose formula for the withdrawal of the strike notices, the continuation of the subsidy for a fortnight and a settlement 'on the lines of the [Samuel] Report' within this period had been worked out. J. H. Thomas, at least, went home that night convinced that agreement was in sight and the strike was off. The TUC representatives were to consult both their General Council and the miners the next morning. As the formula clearly involved some reduction in wages, this was much more than a formality. But Thomas's confidence was not foolish. He knew the mood of the TUC, his own prowess at wheedling persuasion, and the need of the miners for outside support.

What he did not know was that the Government, by the next day, would be anxious to retreat from the formula, and that the miners' executive, having dispersed itself from London, would give them all day in which to do so. Baldwin slept badly and briefly, uncertain about the wisdom or precision of his nocturnal negotiations. When he emerged the next morning he found not uncertainty but widespread consternation. His own staff were dismayed. The Chief Whip thought the party would revolt. Steel-Maitland regretted his share in the discussions. When the Cabinet met at noon, Baldwin found himself sharing a defensive corner with Birkenhead. Hankey told Tom Jones that he had never before witnessed a Cabinet scene like it. 'All who were not present when [the formula] was agreed reacted in the same way against it, and felt that it would be read by the whole country as a capitulation on the part of the Government to the threat of a General Strike.'[10]

The Cabinet met twice again before dinner time, and on each occasion moved themselves into a harder position. By the time that Baldwin again met the TUC representatives, at 9 p.m., he was, by the will of the Cabinet, a long way back from the position of the previous night, and embarrassed by the movement. To extricate himself he had to fasten on the strike notices which the TUC had sent out and demand their unconditional withdrawal as a prelude to further negotiations. By the time the miners arrived at 11.30, there was nothing urgent to discuss with them. Then came the news that the *Daily Mail* compositors had refused to set an offending leading article. Joynson-Hicks announced this to the Cabinet as though it were the end of constitutional government. The Cabinet in turn chose to treat it as the beginning of the General Strike.* At 1.15 a.m. (becoming a favourite time) Baldwin again saw the TUC and 'with great regret' in effect dismissed them.

The next day there were only perfunctory contacts. Baldwin spoke in the House of Commons in the afternoon, conciliatory in form, firm in substance. The strike was a challenge to constitutional government. As such it must be resolutely resisted. It began on Tuesday morning, 4 May. The Prime Minister greeted the day in a much calmer mood than he had forty-eight hours before. He had got himself into a difficult position and had escaped with more luck than dignity. He had not avoided a strike, which was half his inclination, but he had preserved a reasonably favourable position, both for himself and for resistance.

The General Strike lasted eight days. Baldwin's main rôle was to keep his colleagues and the country as calm as possible. Churchill was the principal firebrand. Baldwin shunted him to the editorship of the official *British Gazette*, 'to stop him doing worse things', but at the same time kept control over what was published by the remarkable feat of giving Davidson, a junior minister at the Admiralty, some real power of censorship over what the Chancellor of the Exchequer wrote. He declined to take the Home Secretary's advice to close down the *Daily Herald*, and declined also to allow Churchill to take over the BBC. This was an act of the most palpable commonsense, for John Reith,* the Manager, was willing to give the cloak of

* Baldwin's principal private secretary got the King's secretary out of bed at Windsor to tell him the dread news. 'The *Daily Mail* has ceased to function,' he announced, at once portentously and ambiguously. 'Tell His Majesty so that he should not go off the deep end.' At Windsor there was a greater sense of proportion. 'We don't take the *Daily Mail*, or the *Daily Express*, Sir Clive Wigram said sleepily, and rang off. (Tom Jones, *A Diary with Letters*, page 133.)

independence to everything that the Government wanted. He even postponed, on his own responsibility, a proposal for a mediatory broadcast by the Archbishop of Canterbury (Randall Davidson), which the Government itself would have found very difficult to forbid. On at least one issue, however, Baldwin failed to give any firm moderate lead. This was the proposal to rush punitive trade union legislation through Parliament while the strike was in progress. The Cabinet came very near to such a decision. Jones, although supported by most official opinion, failed for once to influence Baldwin directly. Eventually, a combination of the King and Conservative backbench opinion, both more cautious than the Prime Minister, secured a deflection. The legislation was postponed for nearly a year.

In his own direct wireless appeal to the public Baldwin applied more characteristic tactics. He did not broadcast himself until the Saturday evening (8 May), and then used much less provocative language than most of his colleagues would have chosen. The end even reads rather plaintively, but was no doubt saved by his resonant broadcasting voice:

> I am a man of peace. I am longing, and looking and praying for peace. But I will not surrender the safety and the security of the British Constitution. It placed me in power eighteen months ago by the largest majority accorded to any party for many, many years. Have I done anything to forfeit that confidence? Cannot you trust me to ensure a square deal and to ensure even justice between man and man?

He stressed throughout the difference between the coal strike, which was industrial and could be negotiated, and the General Strike, which was aimed at the constitution and must be defeated unconditionally. But he interpreted defeat in a quiet way. 'We must wait for the strike to wear itself out,' was his private summary of his tactics.[11] He did not have to wait very long. At midday on Wednesday, 12 May, the TUC surrendered. Baldwin said, 'I thank God for your decision,' and

applied himself to mediating in the coal dispute which continued independently.

At first he showed some energy, but as recalcitrance persisted on both sides this quickly exhausted itself. By the end of
May he could see no way forward. Then he put through a bill to
suspend for five years the Seven Hours Act, which had restricted maximum daily hours for the coal industry since 1919,
following the Eight Hours Act of 1908. It was no solution (as
well as being contrary to Samuel) and brought the miners no
nearer to working any hours at all. But it gave the owners an
unfortunate concession for the future. The Government, while
proclaiming itself doctrinally reluctant to impose a settlement
upon the industry, had caused Parliament to pronounce upon a
major issue in the dispute. Although in return the Yorkshire
owners were privately pushed off a proposal for a more grasping division of profits and wages, the Government refrained
from balancing the bill by any enforcement of minimum wages
or national arbitration.

By the second week in July Baldwin felt able to say nothing
more constructive about the ten-week-old lock-out than
'Leave it alone – we are all so tired.' On 10 August Neville
Chamberlain noted: 'S.B. has suffered most from the strike; he
too is worn out and has no spirit left, but he remains the one
with the greatest influence in the country.'[12] On the latter
point the King felt the same confidence, although less reluctantly, and reacted to it with some lack of consideration by
more or less commanding Baldwin not to leave the country for
his annual expedition to Aix. It was a pointless 'command', for
Baldwin was on the edge of nervous collapse, irritable, complaining and, in the closer judgment of Jones, "entirely without resource". The Downing Street secretaries circumvented
the King by getting an haphazardly chosen doctor* (they had

---

* He sounds like an opera character, got up for the part: 'On his arrival at No 10
[Waterhouse] briefed him fully as to the P.M.'s symptoms and as to what we
Secretaries wished should be done. S.B. himself had no idea who or what sort of
specialist the doctor was. The doctor played up splendidly . . .' (Jones, A Diary with
Letters, page 64).

previously tried fourteen others, all of whom were away) to come in and certify that the Prime Minister had to go. Baldwin left for Aix on 22 August, and stayed away until 15 September.

During this period Churchill took over the coal negotiations and displayed a vigour for settlement which had been entirely lacking in the Prime Minister. Also, and in sharp contrast with his attitude during the General Strike, he exhibited consider-able sympathy for the miners. As his series of meetings pro-gressed, some at Chartwell, some in London, there was even fear on the part of Jones and Davidson that he might get a settlement in the absence of the Prime Minister and thus damage Baldwin's position. The fear was misplaced. Obduracy was too great. The Cabinet was stubborn as well as the owners. They both felt, rightly, that the miners were close to being starved into submission and saw little reason to interfere with this elegant process. The last possible moment for a negotiated settlement was in the third week of September. Churchill then wanted to coerce the owners into a national agreement and statutory arbitration. Baldwin was half with him, but was 'suffering from sciatica and obviously did not know which way to turn in the midst of his conflicting advisers'.[13] The Cabinet turned them both down and decided to do nothing. Birken-head said it was the most difficult decision since the evacuation of the Dardanelles, but that did not help much. The decision would probably have gone the other way had 100,000 men not already been back at work, mainly in the more prosperous East and West Midland areas.

The policy of inactivity had to be defended in the House of Commons in the following week. Baldwin did so flatly and uncomfortably. Churchill put a bolder and more sympathetic face upon his speech: 'During the brilliant performance the P.M.'s face was turned towards the Official Gallery, and co-vered with one of his hands. He looked utterly wretched, much as Ramsay does when L.G. is on his legs.'[14] Thus, according to Jones, did Baldwin both reap the harvest of inactivity and exhibit an unusual burst of jealousy.

In October the Nottinghamshire miners formed a breakaway union and went back to work. In November the strike finally collapsed. In December the majority of the men were back at work, with lower wages, an eight-hour day, and with a substantial minority condemned to permanent unemployment. They were cowed and bitter, with the Miners' Federation weakened for a decade. The national cost had been heavy. At a time when the national income was little more than £2 billion* a coal production loss of nearly £100 million and a total loss of nearly £250 million had been incurred. Whole communities were alienated and impoverished; a large part of the nation was left with a feeling halfway between guilt and unease; and Baldwin's reputation as a statesman of sagacious moderation was badly dented. The General Strike was one thing. That he was widely felt to have handled well. He had calmly upheld the supremacy of the state. The coal strike was another. In dealing with that he failed to show sustained energy, or to make effective and impartial use of the authority of the state, the importance of which he had so insistently proclaimed in May.

On the other hand, at a heavy price, he had secured a substantial victory for the conservative forces in British life. He had decisively taken the edge off trade union power. The days lost in strikes rapidly fell to a much lower level than at any time since 1918. At the 1928 Trades Union Congress Cook and the other left-wing members were defeated by a majority of more than two to one. The so-called Mond-Turner talks, leading to little in themselves, but symbolizing a more cooperative approach, became possible. The transition to the trades unionism of the 1930s, to the Bevin-Citrine era of involvement in the processes of government, had begun. The trouble was that Baldwin did it by the methods he had foresworn and that his words and his style of appeal had become alienated from his actions. He went on talking of peace, but he had become a man who had allowed Britain's major industry to be decimated and embittered.

* As against approximately £300 billion in 1986.

CHAPTER FIVE

The Defeat of 'Safety First'

Nineteen twenty-nine was necessarily an election year. The Cabinet had a full discussion of the date as early as October 1928, but left unresolved the issue of summer or autumn. Baldwin inclined to the earlier date, mainly because he always sustained himself throughout the wearisomeness of the political year by looking forward to a relaxed August and September. 'We should be campaigning all through the holidays after a hard session,' he commented gloomily on the October proposal.[1] The winter and early spring brought bad by-election results from the Conservatives, but the earlier date was nevertheless decided upon. Polling day was 30 May.

Baldwin firmly believed that he would win. He realized that he was short on programme, but thought that his reputation as a moderate statesman, calmly if slowly steering the country in the right direction, would overcome that. The Liberals were strongest on policy. The Keynesian Yellow Book, fortified by a sharp and confident pamphlet, *We Can Conquer Unemployment*, gave them that. The Labour Party had Ramsay MacDonald's voice and presence, the loyalty of much of the bunkered working class, and a manifesto which avoided both the advantages and disadvantages of precision. Baldwin had accepted the slogan of 'Safety first', made familiar by a Ministry of Transport motoring campaign and proposed to the Conservative Central Office by an advertising agency. With unemployment at 10 per cent it was hardly inspired. And he had to spend a good part of the campaign explaining that it meant caution and not com-

placency. Nevertheless the campaign strengthened his optimism. He was very well received in his speaking expeditions,
particularly in Lancashire, and he returned confidently to
Downing Street to await the results.

In those days few ministers thought it necessary to attend
their own counts, and Baldwin had his vigil in the No. 10
secretaries' room enlivened by the presence of Churchill: 'The
P.M. [sat] with narrow slips of paper on which he inscribed the
three lists as they arrived. At [another] desk sat Winston doing
similar lists in red ink, sipping whisky and soda, getting redder
and redder, rising and going out often to glare at the machine
himself, hunching his shoulders, bowing his head like a bull
about to charge.' Baldwin took the defeat less aggressively: but
'he found it hard to reconcile the results with the reception on
tour.'[2]

The result was not a disaster, but it was a severe setback for
the Conservatives. They dropped 150 seats. The main effect of
the strong Liberal campaign was to put Labour candidates in on
minority votes. The Liberals themselves secured only 59 seats.
The Labour Party won 287, the Government 261. Baldwin's
first problem was whether to resign at once, or, as in 1923, to
wait and meet Parliament. The situation was different, because
the Conservatives had then been the largest party, whereas
they were now 26 seats behind the Labour Party. There was
nevertheless strong pressure for hanging on. This was the view
of the two Chamberlains, of the Chief Whip (Eyres-Monsell•),
and, at first, of Churchill. Baldwin retired to Chequers, hesitated, and then decided otherwise. He thought that to remain
would look 'unsporting' and would count against him the next
time. He resigned on 4 June, five days after the poll.

The transition was then less abrupt than has since become
the habit. On 14 June Baldwin was still living in 10 Downing
Street, MacDonald having helpfully retired for a post-election
holiday at Lossiemouth. Baldwin had some considerable
difficulty about finding another place to live. His relative
impoverishment had proceeded rapidly during the twenties.

Baldwins Ltd's shares were only at 3/6. The loss of his Prime Minister's salary was a serious matter, and he refused to take either to journalism or the City, as he had criticized Lloyd George for one and Sir Robert Horne for the other. He talked about selling Astley and although it was probably little more than talk, he was forced to run it extremely economically, and could not think of another London house on the scale of Eaton Square. Eventually he took a short lease on a much smaller house in Upper Brook Street.

His main summer objective, as usual, was to get through to his holiday. This he accomplished satisfactorily. The defeat, as was natural, led to a good deal of rumbling, particularly against the Conservative Central Office, where Davidson, the Chairman since 1927, was far too much Baldwin's own man to be a satisfactory lightning conductor. But at first these rumblings were mainly subterranean. A Central Council meeting on 2 July passed off with some display of enthusiasm, and gave Baldwin a unanimous vote of confidence. His own speech was skilful in detail, but highly defensive in concept. He was in France for six weeks in August and September and then had another two or three weeks staying with friends in the North of England and Scotland. He did not make a settled return to London until 20 October. Then, for the eighteen months until March 1931, he experienced one of the roughest passages which has been the lot of any party leader this century.

The trouble was three-fold. First, he had no taste and little ability for the harrying of a government. He constantly ignored Bolingbroke's maxim that Members of Parliament are like hounds that grow fond of the leader 'who shows them game and by whose halloo they are used to be encouraged.'[3] Indeed, at Sheffield in May 1930 he almost erected the contrary view into a principle:

I hold the view very strongly – and I know I have been criticised for it – that when a government has not got great experience, is a minority government, it is essential if you can possibly support it that it should be able to speak with a strong voice to the countries of the world.

As a result the MacDonald Government, despite its many faults and vicissitudes, was left almost miraculously free from strong and sustained attack by its principal opponent. All Baldwin's notable speeches of this period, both in the House and in the country, were devoted to troubles within his own party. When occasionally he rather wearily turned on the Government, the reaction was one of surprise more than of dismay.

Second, he was subjected to a sustained attack by the two principal popular newspaper proprietors of the day, Beaverbrook* and Rothermere.* The point nominally at issue was the one which had spasmodically rent the Conservative Party for the past three decades – the tariff question. The intricacies of this had almost defied analysis since the early years of the century when Balfour had deliberately muddied the waters. Safeguarding, retaliation, imperial preference, protection for industry but not for agriculture, all created a web of almost infinite complexity. It was very difficult to remember who had been for what at which particular period. Indeed it can be argued that none of this greatly mattered. The issue flared up when the party was doing badly for other reasons, and subsided when it was not.

It was the classic recipe for embarrassing a leader. And the two press lords, and some others, certainly wished to embarrass Baldwin. Had the issue been treated seriously he ought to have been more than usually invulnerable upon it. No one had risked more for tariff reform than he had in 1923. But Rothermere and Beaverbrook were not principally interested in the issue for its own sake. Rothermere, indeed, hardly cared about it at all. He hated Baldwin and that was enough. Beaverbrook had some genuine concern, and was less consistently anti-Baldwin. But he loved mischief, and he rarely considered whether his schemes made sense. He committed himself to a singularly foolish plan for Empire Free Trade. It was singularly foolish because it obviously could not work without reciprocity, and no Dominion leader, not even his erstwhile friend Bennett of Canada, was willing to throw their markets open to British goods. Rothermere, a much bigger newspaper owner, supported Beaverbrook in uneasy alliance. The Empire Crusade was designed to cause the maximum trouble for the Conservative leadership. Its promoters took the extreme step of running independent Conservative candidates in by-elections. They won one, in South Paddington, and cost official Conservative candidates the seat in several more, often driving them into third place.

This would at best have been a major irritant for an embattled leader of the opposition. But it became worse than that. Neville Chamberlain was the most likely alternative leader. He, it was rightly thought, would provide the drive and the partisan bitterness which were lacking in Baldwin's style. On the whole he was loyal to Baldwin, whom he liked to describe, with a degree of exaggeration, as his friend as well as his leader. But he was ambitious, in addition to being sixty, and he did not wish to hang about indefinitely under an ineffective leader. Furthermore, despite a vast difference in temperament, he was surprisingly close to Beaverbrook in this period, both in view and in personal dealings. Most of the anti-Baldwin rebels looked to him as their natural leader, and he was unanxious to alienate their support, which, wherever he showed signs of excessive caution or loyalty, began to move towards substitutes. Rothermere was in favour of Beaverbrook himself, and Hailsham• and Robert Horne (a surprising revival as he had been out of office since the Coalition) also emerged as occasional possibilities; pace 1923, no one seemed inclined to disqualify peers. The tariff issue was therefore full of danger for Baldwin, not so much because of its content as because it could be exploited by those who wished to build up discontent against the spirit of 'Safety first'.

This discontent was fortified by Baldwin's third trouble – his attitude to India. Irwin, one of his closest political friends and the Viceroy whom he had himself appointed, declared in October 1929 in favour of Dominion status as the ultimate goal. Baldwin was determined to support him. This was partly because of personal regard and partly because he saw that the moment for choice in India had come. Irwin, or any Viceroy, had by the end of the twenties only two possibilities before him: either to follow, for as long as British willpower and resources lasted, an unending road of remorseless repression, or to parley, more or less as an equal, with Gandhi and his adjutants with a view to guiding the country, maybe fairly slowly but nonetheless unrelentingly, towards self-government. Baldwin and Irwin both believed in accommodation and not in confrontation. They were Conservatives in the sense that the Halifax of 1633–95 (no relation of Irwin's), who proudly bore the titles both of marquess and of 'trimmer', was a Conservative.

The policy they embraced was however anathema to many Conservatives, who rightly saw in it the beginning of the end of British rule in India. There was some considerable overlapping with those who were harrying Baldwin by their support of the Empire Crusade, but it was by no means complete. The most notable maverick was Churchill, who retained most of his old free trade views, but was implacably opposed to progress in India. In January 1931 he left the Shadow Cabinet on the issue and did not return to communion with the official Conservative leadership until after the outbreak of war in 1939.

These two areas of dispute sustained and fortified each other throughout the eighteen months of Baldwin's unease. If one was quiet, the other was active. He always had a battle pending on one front and quite often on two at the same time. He was mostly on the defensive and, towards the end, he came as near as possible to resignation, but throughout he gave remarkably little ground on either issue. His first choice was to remain leader on his own terms, his second to go, and his third, last, and unacceptable one was to cling to the position on the terms of others. By virtue of this settled view he managed to live tolerably through the period, to risk his fate in a number of bold throws, and to emerge at the end with his dignity unimpaired and his power enhanced. He liked to believe that he never sought conflict. To Beaverbrook, however, he appeared in a different light. 'He always won,' Beaverbrook said, 'he always beat me – the toughest and most unscrupulous politician you could find – cold, merciless in his dislikes.'[4]

During the successive rounds of these twin controversies Baldwin used with remarkable freedom the House of Commons as well as public platforms to carry on the debate within his own party. The first exchange came at the beginning of November 1929. At a Shadow Cabinet meeting he found that the Viceroy's declaration was strongly opposed by his three most senior colleagues, Austen Chamberlain, Birkenhead and Churchill. The next morning the *Daily Mail* launched a vicious attack upon him, injudiciously using false facts as well as offering opinions. That afternoon in the Chamber the article was referred to in a question exchange. Baldwin rose briefly and magisterially: 'It is sufficient for me at the moment to say that every statement of fact and every implication of fact in that article is untrue, and in my opinion gravely injurious to the public interest, not only in the country but throughout the Empire.'

A few days later there was a major debate on the Irwin declaration. Baldwin, with a glowering Churchill beside him and uncertain followers behind him, took the opportunity to pay a notable tribute to the Viceroy and to end it on a curious note, half petulant, half menacing: 'I will only add that if ever the day comes when the party which I lead ceases to attract to itself men of the calibre of Edward Wood, then I have finished with my party.'[4] He then launched into one of his ruminative orations, reflecting on the evolution of our relations with India, hardly engaging with the Government at all, but indirectly committing himself to full support for the movement towards self-government. The informed diehards were affronted, but

the majority of the Conservative Members felt that the level of
the occasion had been raised, and cheered appreciatively. For
the moment he was on top on India.

There then followed a winter of rather confused but relatively quiet negotiation, manoeuvre, and attempt at compromise on the tariff issue. Relations even with Beaverbrook were
still nominally bland and Baldwin was endeavouring to hold
everybody together by steering a middle course between
Amery and Churchill, who within the Shadow Cabinet re-
spectively represented the two extremes. In a March speech at
the Hotel Cecil he laid down a plan of submitting food taxes –
the most controversial item – to a referendum. It offended
nobody but like most policies which achieve that result, it did
not greatly please anyone either. Baldwin's spring campaign
went rather flat. Several Conservative candidates in by-
elections – egged on by Beaverbrook – went well beyond the
official policy and as a result got little official support. In the
meantime discontent with the Central Office – which was
mostly an excuse for discontent with the leadership – continued to mount. In April Neville Chamberlain had told Davidson he must give up his post as party Chairman. Weak for once,
Baldwin accepted this, and let his henchman resign on 29 May.
After casting around a little, he appointed Chamberlain himself
in Davidson's place.

Baldwin then counterattacked by calling a party meeting –
MPs and candidates but no peers – at the Caxton Hall for 24
June. There he delivered the first of his attacks upon the press
lords: 'There is nothing more curious in modern evolution than
the effect of an enormous fortune rapidly made and the control
of newspapers of your own. The three most striking cases are
Mr Hearst in America, Lord Rothermere in England and Lord
Beaverbrook. . . .' He turned on Rothermere in particular,
citing his tergiversations and saying contemptuously, 'You
cannot take your politics from a man like that.' Then he quoted
a letter which Rothermere had been foolish enough to
write:

'I cannot make it too abundantly clear that, under no circumstances whatsoever, will I support Mr Baldwin unless I know exactly what his policy is going to be, unless I have complete guarantees that such policy will be carried out if his party achieves office, and unless I am acquainted with the names of at least eight or ten of his most prominent colleagues in the next Ministry.'

Now there are terms [Baldwin continued] that your leader would have to accept, and when sent for by the King would have to say: 'Sire, these names are not necessarily my choice, but they have the support of Lord Rothermere.' A more preposterous and insolent demand was never made on the leader of any political party. I repudiate it with contempt and I will fight that attempt at domination to the end.

Baldwin did not confine himself to Rothermere:

'We are told that unless we make peace with these noblemen, candidates are to be run all over the country. The Lloyd George candidates at the last election smelt; these will stink. The challenge has been issued. . . . I accept, as I accepted the challenge of the T.U.C. . . . I am all for peace. I like the other man to begin the fight and then I am ready. When I fight I go on to the end, as I did in 1926.'

The vote at the meeting was not very satisfactory – about 150 to 80 against an anti-leadership amendment – but Baldwin's riposte to provocation met with a wide response. He was tumultuously cheered in the House of Commons that afternoon, although a good part of the enthusiasm came from the Labour benches.

This at least got him through to another summer holiday, but while he was away there was a further worsening. The Empire Crusade ran its first independent candidate at the Bromley by-election. This candidate did respectably rather than brilliantly. He was third, but only 3000 behind the winner and almost put in the Liberal in what should have been one of the safest Conservative seats in the country. Nor did this rebellion have the effect of rallying the Conservative faithful. On the contrary, it led to a significant wave of resignations by constituency officers and cancelled subscriptions, particularly in the South of England. And it was to be followed in October by a second and still more menacing contest in another safe seat, South Paddington.

As a result of all this, Baldwin found himself back in the Caxton Hall by 30 October. He deliberately chose the day to coincide with the Paddington election. If he was to have two bad results he might as well let them merge. If, on the other hand, the party meeting were to go well for him, it would be a helpful antidote to a bad by-election. And if both went well, he might acquire a momentum of success. In fact, as he probably expected, the Caxton Hall meeting went excellently and Paddington went very badly. Beaverbrook's candidate beat the official Conservative in a straight fight.

This Caxton Hall meeting was more serious than the previous one. It was a full meeting of MPs and peers, and assembled to determine the future of the leadership. Baldwin encouraged it to do so – by inviting an unacceptable resolution, by promoting a secret ballot, and letting it be known that he would resign if defeated. He arrived in a top hat and morning coat, already a somewhat archaic form of working dress, and said to the waiting cameraman: 'Photograph me now, gentlemen, it may be the last time you will see me.'

He made only a brief speech to the meeting, described by Bridgeman to Davidson (who was in the Argentine) as 'a good opening – plain and dignified – and with fewer mannerisms than have recently been apparent, and no apparent nervousness'. Baldwin then immediately left the meeting with what he self-mockingly described as '*hauteur*'. The debate dragged on in his absence and he had to wait nearly three hours for the result. It gave him a majority of 462 to 116.

That, even with the loss of Paddington, ought to have been

that on the tariff issue for some time. But within a fortnight the Indian Round Table Conference had opened in London, and the second fissiparous issue had filled any gap left by the temporary subsidence of the first. Churchill began his campaign on 12 December before the Royal Empire Society with an onslaught on Dominion Status as 'a hideous act of self-mutilation astounding to every nation in the world'; continued it for a more general audience by personally hiring the Free Trade Hall in Manchester; and moved inexorably towards his Shadow Cabinet resignation at the end of January. This was precipitated by a House of Commons debate, marked by calculating and outrageous invective by Churchill, and by a less than usually effective speech from Baldwin.* Even Hoare (later to be Baldwin's most loyal lieutenant on India) complained of its clumsiness, and Neville Chamberlain was even more critical.

In February an Empire Crusade candidate beat the official Conservative into third place at East Islington, and left Labour holding what ought to have been a very vulnerable seat for the Government. Then Robert Topping,• the Conservative Chief Agent, drew up and presented to Chamberlain a memorandum saying that 'from practically all quarters' he heard the view that the leader ought to go. This document, which was rich in wounding phrases, was by no means unwelcome to Chamberlain, particularly as it ended with a fairly clear hint that he ought to be the new leader. He then behaved somewhat unctuously, showing it to half the Shadow Cabinet in order to get their advice as to whether or not he ought to worry Baldwin with it. Eventually he sent it to Baldwin immediately after the latter had received a further damaging and depressing blow. The St George's Division of Westminster had fallen vacant in early February. It was an overwhelmingly Conservative seat, made up in large part of Mayfair and Belgravia. But it was also very favourable ground for Beaverbrook and Rothermere, who

---

* Its only memorable passage was when he took up a previous reference to the loss of the American Colonies and said that 'If George III had been endowed with the tongue of Edmund Burke for only an hour, he might have made such a speech [as Churchill]' (Hansard, vol. 247, col. 744, 26 Jan. 1931).

already had an organization in the field. When they adopted a candidate – one Sir Ernest Petter – the official Conservative candidate, Colonel Moore-Brabazon,• at once withdrew. The gallant colonel did not wish to defend his leader. This was not only humiliating but also very awkward for Baldwin. It was not going to be easy to get any other candidate, and it was at the same time impossible to let the seat go by default.

This was Baldwin's position when he received the Topping memorandum. Cunliffe-Lister brought it, together with the news that the Chief Whip had sounded out his principal colleagues upon it and that they all thought he ought to resign. Baldwin, with his wife, then saw Davidson, and although 'still a little stunned' they both talked in terms of an immediate and complete withdrawal to Astley. That afternoon (it was all on a Sunday) he saw Chamberlain, and having directly asked him whether he agreed with the others and having received an affirmative answer, told him to call a meeting of the Shadow Cabinet for the following day at which he would say goodbye.

The same evening Davidson dined with Bridgeman. The latter, contrary to the expressed view of the Chief Whip, was aghast at the prospect of resignation. Together they went to see Baldwin after dinner and persuaded him, apparently without great difficulty, to go out, if he had to, with a bang and not a whimper. Why not resign Bewdley and fight St George's himself? Baldwin rallied with enthusiasm. He summoned Chamberlain to see him again first thing the next morning and told him his new plan. It was then Chamberlain's turn to be aghast. He remonstrated strongly against the plan to fight St George's. 'Think of the effect upon your successor,' he tactlessly argued. Baldwin, for the moment, had had enough of Chamberlain. 'I don't give a damn about my successor, Neville,' he said and ended the conversation.[6]

In fact he did not fight the bye-election. Duff Cooper,• an improbable standard-bearer, for he had acclaimed the victory of the independent candidate in Paddington and his wife was a close friend of Beaverbook, offered himself as a knightly substitute; and Baldwin, who did not want to sever his connection with Bewdley, accepted gratefully. But he still regarded the result as crucial and in no way retreated from his new-found determination to fight. He got the pending Indian debate brought foward a week to 12 March and took little counsel about the form of his speech, although receiving plenty of advice from his colleagues to strike a conciliatory note.

He did nothing of the sort. He sharply reminded his party that 'The Empire of today is not the Empire of the first Jubilee of Queen Victoria'; he had some effective fun at Churchill's expense; he strongly defended the 'Delhi Pact' between Irwin and Gandhi; and he ended on a note of clear challenge:

> If there are those in our party who approach this subject in a niggling, grudging spirit, who would have to have forced out of their reluctant hands one concession after another, if they be a majority, in God's name let them choose a man to lead them. If they are in a minority, then let them at least refrain from throwing difficulties in the way of those who have undertaken an almost superhuman task, on the successful fulfilment of which depends the well being, the prosperity and the duration of the whole British Empire.[7]

The speech was a triumph. The 1929 Parliament was hardly the most glorious in our history, but it was still one in which it was possible to face a major issue on its merits, and to debate with one's own party without producing mindless noise or mockery from the other side, and by so doing to create an impact upon the general body of the House which improved – and in this instance strikingly improved – the position of the speaker with his own party. But Baldwin still had St George's to face – polling day was a week later, and Baldwin spoke twice in the interval, once at the Queen's Hall, and again the following night at the Constitutional Club. The first speech was much the more important: it was indeed one of the most memorable of inter-war political orations. It contained some routine passages but the central message was a sustained attack upon the two press lords:

> The papers conducted by Lord Rothermere and Lord Beaverbrook are not newspapers in the ordinary acceptance of the term. They are engines of propaganda for the constantly changing policies, desires, personal wishes, personal likes and dislikes of two men. What are their methods? Their methods are direct falsehood, misrepresentation, half-truths, the alteration of the speaker's meaning by publishing a sentence apart from the context. . . .

He cited a *Daily Mail* article, rather curiously signed Editor, which had attacked him for presiding over the disappearance of 'an immense fortune' left him by his father, and had concluded: 'It is difficult to see how the leader of a party who has lost his own fortune can hope to restore those of anyone else, or his country.'

Baldwin then castigated the 'Editor' in what now seems rather old-fashioned but nonetheless devastating terms:

> I have no idea of the name of the gentleman. I would only observe that he is well qualified for the post which he holds. The first part of the statement is a lie and the second part of the statement by its implications is untrue. The paragraph itself could only have been written by a cad. I have consulted a very high legal authority and am advised that an action for libel would lie. I shall not move in the matter, and for this reason: I should get an apology and heavy damages. The first is of no value, and the second I would not touch with a barge pole. What the proprietorship of these papers is aiming at is power, and power without responsibility − the prerogative of the harlot throughout the ages . . . this contest is not a contest as to who is to lead the party, but as to who is to appoint the leader of the party.

Duff Cooper, against all expectations of a few weeks before, won by a majority of nearly 6000. This was the end of the tunnel for Baldwin. Nineteen days after the Sunday when he was deemed to have no alternative than to resign in ignominy his leadership was more secure than at any time since the 1929 election. Neville Chamberlain was still lamenting that Baldwin did not attack the Government instead of the press lords. A concordat of a sort had to be arranged with him, and this was done with mutual protestations that only misunderstanding had impaired goodwill. Chamberlain also believed that he had arranged a mini-concordat of his own with Beaverbrook.* The Empire Crusade continued in existence (indeed its symbol still decorates the front page of the *Daily Express*), but like many of Beaverbrook's enterprises, it quickly faded from his attention and that of the country. And Austen Chamberlain was still telling Baldwin that the Conservative position would only be restored if he bestirred himself and put a less negative spirit in his speeches. One of Baldwin's weaknesses in dealing with his colleagues was that, at least until after 1931, he inspired no awe. In public he could be magisterial. But in private he affected too much modesty, and before 1922 had been junior to too many of them.

All this, however, did little to impair his triumph. He could approach the cataclysmic events of the forthcoming August with an adequate authority; and he could in the future look back on 1931 with a certain complacency, as 'the year my party tried to get rid of me'.[8] They tried, and they failed. They did not try again.

---

* 'I have been overwhelmed with congratulations from all quarters', he wrote about this to his wife, '(except S.B. who can't bear the thought of making it up with the press lords and doesn't see how it has helped his own position)' (quoted in Iain Macleod, *Neville Chamberlain*, page 145).

CHAPTER SIX

The National Government

During the first half of 1931, the prospects of the Labour Government worsened sharply. This may indeed have been an underlying cause of the revival of Baldwin's own fortunes. The lively hope of success is always a good healer for a political party and a prop to the position of its leader. Unemployment, reacting to the world slump and concentrated in the export trades, had risen steadily throughout 1930. By the end of the year it passed the two and a half million mark, just over double the figure when the Government had taken office. For some time MacDonald managed to ride this deterioration with remarkable aplomb. 'It is not our crisis, it is the crisis of capitalism,' he had successfully if unconstructively assured the 1930 Labour Party Conference. But as the figure mounted still further, as it became abundantly clear that the Cabinet was barren of remedy, as the harsh eloquence of Oswald Mosley's• attacks damaged without moving the Government from which he had recently resigned, so comforting oratory became less of a substitute for action. The Labour Party began to lose by-elections, and the performance of the Conservative Party improved substantially even in those seats which did not change hands.

In March 1931 Snowden, the Chancellor of the Exchequer, referred to 'the national position [as being] so grave that drastic and disagreeable measures will have to be taken', and accepted a Liberal amendment to set up an Economy Committee. Under the chairmanship of Sir George May, secretary of the

Prudential Assurance Company, the committee became a time-bomb ticking away under the life of the Government. The Government had asked an outside and unfriendly body to make recommendations upon one of the most sensitive areas of politics. When the recommendations came, the Government, in a prejudiced atmosphere, would have to decide whether or not to accept. The Report was due at the end of July, and as the summer advanced the mounting drain on the insolvent unemployment insurance fund made the issue still more critical.

Before mid-summer Baldwin did not believe that the Government could last beyond the autumn, but he was still hoping that he could get his Aix holiday. The evidence is overwhelming that he did not at this stage contemplate a coalition government. What he expected was to see the Labour Government driven into an election either by its own dissensions or by the action of the Liberals, and its consequent replacement by a Conservative administration, obviously with himself at the head. But he believed that MacDonald had made some soundings in a coalition direction, and in a speech at Hull on 19 July he went out of his way to reject 'the idea that a national government such as existed during the war should be set up in the present difficulties'. Before this speech he had carried Neville Chamberlain with him in such rejection, but a week later, when there had already been a period of some pressure against the pound in the foreign exchange markets, Chamberlain thought that events would 'beat down Baldwin's native instinct against coalition'.[1]

Baldwin knew of the development of Chamberlain's view, and made the major mistake in the circumstances of proceeding with his plans for France and leaving Chamberlain in charge in London. From this may well have followed the whole highly undesirable evolution of British politics in the thirties. It was undesirable not only from a national point of view, but also from Baldwin's own standpoint. The political cataclysm of 1931 undermined his central strategy of the twenties. He had wanted a stable balance in politics, with a large, moderate and 'responsible' Labour Party sharing power, although preferably not on an equal basis, with his own form of Conservatism. This balance, for which he had worked hard and long, he allowed to be destroyed by overreaction to the relatively minor financial crisis of August 1931. It was Baldwin's biggest political mistake.

The result was also disadvantageous for him personally. It gave him four and a half years of power without full responsibility – although he no doubt did not consider that this placed him in the harlot class. For this period he was the leader of the party which gave the Government nine-tenths of its majority, but he was only the third man in the hierarchy. This meant some easing of the burden, which he liked, but it also meant that he was not Prime Minister, which he also liked being, that he did not have Chequers, for which his affection was second only to that of MacDonald, and that his salary as Lord President was £2000 instead of the £5000 which Secretaries of State as well as the Prime Minister were paid. This last was a serious matter, at least until the substantial improvement of the fortunes of Baldwins Ltd in 1934. Altogether it was an expensive holiday for which he crossed to Le Havre on 8 August.

It was not even an uninterrupted holiday. For the Government the culminating crisis began on the morning of 11 August 1931, when MacDonald arrived overnight from Lossiemouth. The problem which confronted the Government arose out of the confluence of two streams of difficulty. July had been a month of international financial upheaval. The trouble began with the inability of the German Government to meet their reparations obligations, and with the intransigence of the French, much greater than that of the Americans or the British, towards giving them relief on politically acceptable terms. Berlin suspended cash payments on 13 July and imposed exchange controls two days later. Then the pressure of exchange speculation was diverted against sterling, vulnerable as a currency presided over by a Labour Government with budgetary troubles.

Over the next three weeks the Bank of England lost about £60 million in gold and foreign exchange. The sum, while considerable, was not enormous. It was the equivalent of about £1500 million at 1980's values, although greater than that in relation to the size of the economy. Nor do the crisis protection measures of putting the bank rate to 3½ per cent on 23 July and 4½ per cent on 30 July sound very desperate today. Any good effect of these moves, however, was more than cancelled by publication, without any accompanying statement of Government policy, of the report of the ill-conceived May Committee on that same penultimate day of July. This forecast a budget deficit of £120 million and recommended expenditure cuts of £97 million, including a saving of £67 million on the unemployed. The House of Commons rose and ministers dispersed on their holidays with little chance of an undisturbed recess. If they were to try to maintain the parity of sterling against gold (which was in accordance with their own instincts as well as with the views of most of their advisors, although not of Keynes) they needed substantial foreign credits and they were unlikely to get these without welfare economies which would disrupt the Cabinet and its parliamentary support.

On the morning of 12 August Baldwin, who had got to Angers in the Loire, was summoned back and arrived early the following day. He saw Chamberlain, then a group of Bank of England directors (Montagu Norman was away) and in the afternoon MacDonald and Snowden. On this last occasion, according to Chamberlain, who was also present, Baldwin 'asked no intelligent question, made no helpful suggestion', which Chamberlain attributed to his desire 'to be gone before he was "drawn into something"'.[2] Whether or not this was a correct explanation of his reticence, it was certainly the case that Baldwin was quickly 'gone'. He was back across the Channel that evening and in Aix, after his habitual tour, on Tuesday 18 August. Chamberlain was deputed to handle all negotiations in his absence, and in particular to attend a meeting of the leaders of the three parties which was fixed for that same Tuesday.

Arrangements for such a meeting clearly presupposed an unusual degree of party collusion, but Baldwin persisted in expecting no new combination. As soon as he got to Aix he wrote to Chamberlain: 'I think in the long view it is all to the good that the Government have to look after their own chickens as they come home to roost, and get a lot of the dirt cleared up before we come in.'[3]

Meanwhile the death throes of the Labour Government were beginning. Wednesday was a day of interminable meetings, during which the split over unemployment benefit between MacDonald and a substantial but fluctuatingly composed group of his Cabinet began to assume its final form. On Thursday there was a series of meetings between the leaders of the Government and the opposition parties, the General Council of the TUC and the National Executive of the Labour Party. That evening Chamberlain telephoned to Baldwin in Aix and told him that he ought to return to London. Baldwin accepted this advice, but he did not reach Victoria Station until the evening of Saturday, 22 August, two days later. In the meantime discussion of a National Government had become open and serious between MacDonald and Snowden and the Conservative and Liberal leaders. It is not clear who first raised the matter.* What is certain is that by the late evening of 21 August Chamberlain had strongly urged this course upon MacDonald. And he did so with the support, not only of Hoare, who was his adjutant in all the talks with the Government, but also of Cunliffe-Lister, Hailsham, Eyres-Monsell and Davidson, the last being brought in as the best means of liaison with Baldwin.

Davidson recorded his own position in his draft memoirs:

> Earlier in the month I had been strongly against any idea of coalition. . . . But the situation was now so

---

* In Middlemas and Barnes, *Baldwin*, it is implied that MacDonald first did so, with an oddly jaunty and inappropriately phrased response to an intervention of Hoare's: 'Well, are you prepared to join the Board of Directors?' (page 623)

critical, and the time for restoring confidence so short, that, very reluctantly, I agreed that each Party must sink its political programme temporarily and combine to pursue an economic policy to save the nation from bankruptcy. What influence I had with S.B. was now used to persuade him of the wisdom of this course.[4]

Davidson had of course great opportunity for influence upon Baldwin, and he used it to the full on this occasion. In the late afternoon of 21 August, he crossed to Paris and joined Baldwin at the Ritz shortly before midnight. They talked until one. The next day he accompanied Baldwin back to London, and upon arrival took him to his house in Westminster. After dinner the leading Conservatives arrived. Davidson's account was as follows:

The discussions at my house that evening were incon-clusive. S.B. was deeply reluctant to envisage a new coalition. He had destroyed one and did not wish to form another. Neville Chamberlain became very im-patient with S.B.'s attitude. He made it quite clear that he could see no other way out of the situation. S.B. agreed that if that was indeed the case it would be his duty to take part in it. It was clear, however, that he was still very worried about the whole idea.[5]

Hoare confirmed this view of Baldwin's state of mind.* Baldwin gave him the impression 'that the last thing in the world that he wished was either a return to office or the end of his holiday. . . . Only if a National Government was really inevitable was he willing to take his part in it. Chamberlain and I were inclined to be impatient when we saw him so reluctant to take the only course which seemed to us possible.'[6]

Baldwin's reluctance had therefore to be set against a for-

---

* The only difference, a surprising but typical example of the frailty of human memory, was that Davidson was convinced the discussion was in his own house, whereas Hoare believed it was at the Conservative Research Department in Old Queen Street.

midable opposition which had been allowed to solidify and organize itself in his absence. He was determined at least to discuss it with his friend Geoffrey Dawson,* the editor of *The Times*, before entering into commitment. The following morning he went to Dawson's house, thereby missing a telephone call from the King's private secretary asking him to go to the Palace before luncheon (it is not clear why the message was not passed on). As a result the King, who was consulting the opposition leaders with MacDonald's approval, saw Samuel before he saw Baldwin. Samuel argued strongly and persuasively in favour of a National as opposed to a purely Conservative Government, and considerably influenced a receptive King.

Baldwin did not get the King's message until he arrived at the Travellers' Club for lunch. He then went to the Palace at three. The King asked him if he would serve in a National Government under MacDonald. Had he been there earlier he might have been asked a less direct question. But once it was asked, his whole character and political stance gave him little alternative but to say 'yes'. He must, in any event, have felt that the pressures were foreclosing the issue against his original instinct. The King recorded that he was 'greatly pleased with Mr Baldwin's readiness to meet the crisis which had arisen, and to sink Party interests for the sake of the Country.'[7] It is only necessary to reverse the meaning of the sentence to realize how difficult it would have been for Baldwin to have given a negative answer. Thus, against his better, earlier judgment, the decisive step was taken towards the damaging decade-long distortion of the political pattern. It came about through a mixture of chance, his own predeliction for holidays, and Neville Chamberlain's effective, narrow-sighted determination.

There still remained the question of whether MacDonald would fill his essential part in the new arrangement. Probably, after the discussions of the Friday evening, there was not much real doubt about the outcome. But it appeared otherwise at the time. That same Sunday, in the evening, there was played out

Baldwin and Neville Chamberlain, Downing Street, August 1931

Baldwin almost resigns: Caxton Hall, 1930

Three doctors in search of a mandate?
Baldwin, MacDonald and John Simon launch
the National Government election campaign, 1931

Reluctant return of world-weary statesman:
Baldwin in Downing Street, 21 August 1935

ldwin with Hoare, July 1935

The King's toy castle: Fort Belvedere

The Duke and Duchess of Windsor, 1937

A farewell present warily given
and quizzically received.
Baldwin's resignation, 1937

A Government in Exile?
Eden as resigned Foreign
Secretary visits the retired
Prime Minister in the South
of France, March 1938

A rather decrepit old man: Baldwin at Astley, summer of 1944

THE NATIONAL GOVERNMENT · 129

in the Cabinet Room the sad farce of waiting for the telegram of conditions for the line of credit from Morgans' in New York, relayed through the Bank of England, and containing when it came the terms which were wanted by MacDonald and Snowden, but which were anathema to half the Cabinet. On that the final split occurred. MacDonald said he would report to the King, and advise a Palace conference of the three party leaders for the following morning. He asked for and received the resignations of his Cabinet; it was not clear whether they included his own.

Later that night MacDonald saw the other party leaders in Downing Street. Davidson, who talked to Baldwin immediately afterwards, recorded as follows:

> It was quite clear that he [MacDonald] intended to resign and that he had no intention of joining in a Coalition, even though the King had urged him to lead one. Neville, however, pressed on him the support in the country that he would bring to such an administration and the effect it would have in restoring confidence. His arguments seemed to have no effect. To every one else at the meeting it seemed quite clear that MacDonald intended to resign, and S.B. returned from it convinced that he would have to form a Government. Nor did he think this a bad thing since, as I had emphasised before, he had little love for Coalitions.[8]

By the next morning MacDonald had changed his mind. In a half-hour audience the King's new National Government was created. Afterwards the three leaders spent an hour and a half agreeing upon heads of terms. These stated explicitly that the Government would last only for the emergency, and that any subsequent elections would be fought not by the Government as a whole but by the parties. Over the next six weeks this decision was gradually and ineluctably reversed.

A small Cabinet of ten – four Conservatives, four former Labour ministers and two Liberals – was quickly set up.

Baldwin became Lord President of the Council and number three in the Cabinet list (Sankey,• the Lord Chancellor, was above him). The only *douceur* which he asked for and obtained was 11 Downing Street. 'It was very comfortable,' he surprisingly recorded, 'and I could always keep my eye on the Prime Minister.'9 More to the point was that it was some compensation for the lower salary. His three Conservative colleagues were Hoare, Cunliffe-Lister and Neville Chamberlain. The last, the real architect of the Government, accepted tenth place in his old post of Minister of Health. After the autumn election, however, he succeeded Snowden as Chancellor, and remained at the Treasury, manifestly the second man in the Conservative Party, for longer than anyone since Lloyd George. His brother Austen, affronted by the lack of respect paid to his seniority, reluctantly accepted the Admiralty outside the Cabinet. Churchill was left out altogether.

Despite these demotions and exclusions there was little trouble with the Conservative Party over the actions which its leaders had taken, inevitably without much consultation. The party was delighted to have got its hands back on to the levers of power and to have smashed the Labour Party in the process. There were a few growls from Amery, who had also been excluded, but not much more. A party meeting carried unanimously a resolution of approval.

There then followed the abandonment of the gold standard, which the Government had been formed to preserve, several weeks of parliamentary rancour, and a dissolution on 7 October for an election on 27 October. The Government had failed to agree on a programme: Baldwin was for protection; Samuel was against it; and MacDonald asked for 'a doctor's mandate'. But they had agreed, contrary to all the intention and undertakings of August, to stick together and to crush the organizationally solid but bewildered and leader-bereft Labour Party by the ruthless exploitation of popular fear. The campaign was far from glorious, audiences were sullen rather than enthusiastic, but the result sensational. At the 1931 election the Labour Party retained only one in six of the seats they had won in 1929. The supporters of the Government totalled 556, of whom 472 were Conservatives. It was the largest Conservative Party which the House of Commons has ever seen. It compared with 338 Conservative members of the 1918 Coalition Parliament and 396 after the 1983 general election. But the result left Baldwin in essentially the position that he had found so objectionable when held by Austen Chamberlain in 1922. He was the leader of by far the largest party, yet he felt committed by the Buckingham Palace arrangement to another Prime Minister. There was however one important difference. Ramsay MacDonald, unlike Lloyd George, was hardly 'that very terrible thing – a dynamic force'. He was soon to become a pathetic old man.

Baldwin himself was also ageing. He was sixty-five in August 1932, the first summer of the National Government, and celebrated his birthday in the midst of the wearisome bargaining of the Ottawa Imperial Preference Conference. He was leading a delegation of remarkable size: no less than seven members of the Cabinet made the six-week trip. Despite this support Baldwin found the heat, the ceremonial and the oratory oppressive, and the atmosphere uninspiring. He often talked about the Empire, but its reality (save only perhaps for India, which he never visited) did not inspire him. He was glad to escape from Ottawa to Aix. Tom Jones found him getting deaf in 1932, and thought this resulted in his missing remarks to an extent which affected his political judgment. Otherwise his physical condition held up remarkably well. During his Aix holiday he could still walk for three or four (and occasionally even for six) hours a day. In England he was much less energetic.

There was no question of MacDonald following Bonar Law's example and giving him Chequers.* He was as addicted to

* Even had the Prime Minister been prepared to renounce it, the terms of the bequest would have given the second refusal to Neville Chamberlain as Chancellor of the Exchequer. The Prime Minister can offer 11 Downing Street to any minister he likes. He is more restricted in the case of Chequers.

its Chiltern charms as was Baldwin himself. They both, to an extent not subsequently equalled until the era of Harold Wilson and Edward Heath, regarded it as the most agreeable perquisite of the premiership. Baldwin thought Astley was too far to go for weekends, and he was too poor at that stage to rent a Home Counties house. Nor did he much approve of subjecting himself to the nervous exhaustion of house parties as other peoples' guest. (A few years later he was to complain about Eden wearing himself out by this frivolity.) He was therefore reduced to spending most of his weekends during the session in what were then the fairly cramped quarters of 11 Downing Street and what, then as more recently, was its unrestful and unrefreshing atmosphere.

Despite this deprivation, and despite the fact that the difference in their age was only a year, he survived the early and mid-1930s much better than did MacDonald. Even so, it took 'Ramshackle Mac' (a *sobriquet* bestowed by his friend Lady Londonderry) a few years after 1931 to achieve the full splendour of his hopelessness. Samuel, who had sharply critical judgment, thought that he presided well over the Cabinet in the first year of the Government, prepared himself carefully for its meetings and prevented 'knots or tangles . . . from being drawn tight'.[10]

Baldwin was an important but fairly silent auxiliary to MacDonald. The composition of the Cabinet, when it returned to a normal size after the 1931 election, was eleven Conservatives, five Liberals and four former Labour ministers. After the Ottawa Agreements provoked the resignation of Snowden and the free trade Liberals in September 1932, the ratio shifted to 12:3:3. In these circumstances the leader of the Conservative Party naturally enjoyed a general influence in the Government greater than normally belongs to anyone other than the Prime Minister. But it would be a mistake to believe that from the beginning Baldwin exercised all the power and merely allowed MacDonald to sit in impotent glory in 10 Downing Street. On ministerial appointments, for instance, while he made

MacDonald change his intentions in a number of cases, he did not do so without occasional complaint from the Prime Minister, and continuing give and take between the two leaders. Any National Labour figure (they had great scarcity value) was absolutely safe in his office. Sankey (the Lord Chancellor) and J. H. Thomas survived longer than would have been likely had they been Conservatives.

In retrospect it looks odd that such a massive Conservative majority should have sustained such an ineffective ex-Labour Prime Minister for so long. Baldwin was crucial to this apparent paradox, both objectively and subjectively. Objectively, he was little more attractive to the Conservatives who were hostile to MacDonaldite mush than was MacDonald himself. Subjectively, Baldwin felt committed to MacDonald for several reasons. First, he thought it an unspoken part of the 1931 bargain that MacDonald should not be discarded as soon as the immediate crisis was over. Second, he regarded MacDonald's name as a considerable asset, both at home and abroad. Certainly MacDonald's international fame was greater than Baldwin's, and there is some evidence that he maintained a certain touch for foreign affairs well after he had lost it domestically.

Baldwin and most Conservatives also felt that they needed MacDonald (and the guise of being a National administration which went with his name) for electoral reasons. The thirties now look the most monolithic political decade of the past 150 years.* The National (or Conservative) majority of 425 seats in October 1931 was reduced only to the very substantial one of 247 in November 1935. It required the outbreak of war and the threatened imminence of defeat to produce the power-sharing of 1940, which led on to the power transference of 1945.

During the decade, to cautious minds at least, it did not so

---

* Its subsequent rival in this respect, the 1950s, was equally dominated by governments of one party, but they were throughout opposed by numerically strong Labour oppositions, which was not the case in the 1930s.

appear. With only a few islands of relief the Government did very badly in by-elections from the autumn of 1933 to the spring of 1935. Swings towards the Labour Party of 20 to 25 per cent were common. On one occasion the swing went to 50 per cent. The most memorable was at Fulham, now a blood-stained political battleground, in October 1933. It was not the biggest swing, but nonetheless a Conservative majority of 14,000 in 1931 turned into a Labour majority of 5000 only two years later. 'It was a nightmare,' Baldwin told G. M. Young, attributing the defeat exclusively to 'the pacifist' issue and using it as a reason for eschewing rearmament in the early days of Hitler.

The 1931 result, of course, left a great deal of room for recoil, but even so, the average of these results, if reflected in a general election, would have produced a substantial Labour majority in the House of Commons. So far from regarding the 1935 result as a foregone conclusion, Baldwin always felt that the choice of date, intermeshed with the fostering of the suitable national mood, was one of his more considerable political challenges.*

In these circumstances MacDonald could not be treated as a cast-off glove – even had it been in Baldwin's nature to do so. Throughout 1932 and 1933 he retained not only the position of Prime Minister but most of the prerogatives of the office as well. Baldwin acted as an unusually influential leader of the House of Commons,† but not as more than that. And at the same time, mainly voluntarily, he devolved a considerable part of his own power to Neville Chamberlain. Baldwin concerned himself with India; with defence (in a somewhat spasmodic way); with those day-to-day issues which assume sudden importance in the life of a Government and then, almost as quickly, lose it again; and with the loose management of the Conservative

---

* By rashly reflecting upon this view in a 1936 House of Commons speech (see pages 159–60 *infra*) he gave his reputation one of the greatest self-inflicted wounds of political history.

† He did not in name occupy this position. Until Churchill no Prime Minister (unless in the Lords) delegated the title. Since Churchill, so rapidly can constitutional habits change, no Prime Minister has thought of not doing so.

Party in the House of Commons. The formulation and coordination of the Conservative contribution to economic, industrial and social policy he left almost entirely to the Chancellor of the Exchequer. The National Government in its first three years thus operated on the curious basis of the Prime Minister depending to an unusual extent on the second man in the Government, and that second man in turn depending to an equally unusual extent upon the second man in his own party. Nevertheless, some approach to a stable internal balance was achieved.

During 1934 this balance began to break up. The deterioration in MacDonald rapidly gathered momentum. Not only his eyesight and his energy, but his memory and the coherence of his mind began to fail. He lost his way in the middle of speeches. In the House of Commons he became an embarrassing joke, and in Downing Street a guarantee of indecision. He clearly could not lead the Government through a general election. This became apparent to others before it did to MacDonald himself. He was not eager to go. In this respect he was no different from greater Prime Ministers, Gladstone before him and Churchill after him, upon whom senility began to descend while they were still in office, except that with him it came when he was ten years or more younger. Eventually, however, MacDonald accepted the inevitable with a reasonable grace. On 16 May 1935 he told the King of his intention to resign.

The King then saw Baldwin on 20 May, and engaged in an active discussion of the shape of the new Cabinet. King George V always had strong views as to who was suitable for which office, and did not hesitate to express them to his Prime Ministers. On this occasion he effectively vetoed the possibility that Hoare might become Viceroy, on the ground that no Secretary of State for India had ever previously gone to Calcutta or Delhi. Hoare became Foreign Secretary instead, with disastrous results.

The changeover of Prime Minister took place quietly on the afternoon of Friday, 7 June, at the beginning of the Whitsun weekend. While Baldwin's succession to Bonar Law in 1923 has been almost overdiscussed, practically no attention has been given to the way in which he slipped in for the third time in 1935. Yet it is a remarkable example of the way in which a Prime Minister may in certain circumstances be appointed almost by accident. MacDonald's assumption throughout the Government and almost up to the last moment was that Baldwin and he would retire together, and that Neville Chamberlain, with the freshness, if not of youth, at least of never having been Prime Minister before, would succeed directly.

This was probably Baldwin's own intention earlier in the Government. It may well have been the desire of many, perhaps a majority, of the Cabinet and the Conservative back-benchers. They certainly wanted a change of style, and probably a sharper one than Baldwin was likely to provide. But they were not consulted. The Cabinet, had it wished, could of course have staged a revolt. But its collective mind was not nearly clear enough for that, and in any event, Chamberlain, embarrassed by his own self-interest, was almost the only minister who was both strong and wholly secure in his own job. So the King, who liked and was used to Baldwin, simply acted on the assumption that he was to succeed and appointed him without question or consultation. There was a certain irony in the fact that one of the first things Baldwin told the King, on taking over from the decrepit MacDonald, was that he himself needed two months' rest.

That year he did not get it. His main task was to prepare for and win a general election. This was complicated but not necessarily made more difficult by a summer and early autumn dominated by the build-up of the dispute between Italy and Abyssinia, the first issue since 1918 to make the threat of European war vivid to the British people. At the end of June the result of the Peace Ballot had been announced. Conducted by the League of Nations Union, this was the most massive private poll ever carried out. Eleven and a half million people

voted, the overwhelming majority in favour of collective security, although three million of those who supported economic
sanctions against an aggressor jibbed at military ones.

Baldwin thought the questions somewhat unrealistically
phrased, but he nonetheless realized that many of those
organizing and participating in the ballot were part of that
middle, public-spirited opinion which he always regarded as an
important part of his natural constituency. Furthermore, the
attachment to collective security, particularly at a time when
an actual aggressor had appeared over the horizon, seemed an
improvement on the almost nihilistic pacifism of 1933 and
1934. Altogether he sensed what Asquith would have called 'a
favourable curve'. He saw the opportunity to play the peace
card and the moderate rearmament card at the same time,
fortified by the prospect that in times of trouble the public
would prefer to vote for an established Government rather
than a peculiarly unknown opposition. He encouraged Hoare
to give a strong lead at Geneva (although at the same time
telling him: 'Keep us out of war; we are not ready for it'[11]), and
ruminating, again at Aix, moved increasingly towards an
autumn election.

He made no announcement until 19 October, and perhaps
did not even close his own mind until no more than a week
earlier, but on 3 October, the same day that the Italian attack
was eventually launched, he went to Bournemouth and for the
first time in seven years addressed the Conservative Party
Conference.* It was an obvious pre-election speech, skilfully
directed both to his immediate audience and to the less committed outside public. 'Spoke for an hour and had a good
ovation,' Tom Jones wrote. 'Denounced the isolationists, reconciled the Party to the League by supporting rearmament,
and reconciled the pacifists to rearmament by supporting the
Covenant.'[12]

A month later, with polling day only two weeks away,

---

* It was also the last occasion on which he discharged this unwelcome duty. In 1936
the task was delegated to Neville Chamberlain.

Baldwin took the lucky chance of a long-standing 'non-political' engagement to address the Peace Society in the Guildhall and used the occasion to tilt the balance in a still more pacific direction. It was one of the last of his evocative flights of homespun philosophy. There was a lot of 'this dear, dear land of ours', of 'the level evening sun over an English meadow', of 'the rooks tumbling noisily home into the elms', but there was also a good ringing pledge in which the ambiguity, although present, was neither obvious nor too clever by half. 'I give you my word', he said, 'that there will be no great armaments.' A correspondent of *The Times* thought it was 'like the first hearing of a great symphony', and Harold Laski, never one to be outdone in either flattery or hyperbole, wrote to Baldwin that it was 'the greatest speech a Prime Minister has ever made'.[13]

Discounting such judgments of the moment, it is clear that Baldwin fought skilfully, and certain that he fought successfully. It was his tenth general election, his fifth as party leader, and as successful as any. He was unopposed at Bewdley, and in the country as a whole, while losing a hundred seats (the minimum which could be expected after 1931), he still secured the second biggest majority of the century. He had a few weeks to bask in the glow of this last electoral achievement, weeks that were only a little marred by the unpleasantness of Cabinet changes* and the difficulties of moving towards a decision on the application of the oil sanction against Italy.

Then, in the middle weeks of December, Baldwin's reputation took the sharpest plunge, to its lowest point, of his whole active career. The Foreign Secretary he had appointed only six months previously, had for some weeks been as exhausted in

---

* The main difficulty came from the dropping of Londonderry (7th Marquess of, 1878–1949) whom Baldwin had moved in June from the Air Ministry to the leadership of the House of Lords. He was a heavy liability on a variety of grounds, and Baldwin was determined to be rid of him. He went with the worst of grace. Such was the lavishness of Londonderry House entertaining (particularly the great eve of the session receptions) that Birkenhead had described him as 'catering his way into the Cabinet'. Once he was out he dropped some of the catering (there was no eve-of-the-session party in December 1935) and devoted himself to writing long letters of reproach to Baldwin.

health as he had become weak on Italian sanctions. Baldwin noticed the former, but not, so he claimed, the latter development. He was delighted that Hoare planned to get away for a holiday in Switzerland. He was always very sympathetic to anyone's need for a holiday. Then it was arranged that Hoare should on the way spend a day or so in Paris talking to Laval, who was temporarily Prime Minister as well as Foreign Minister of France. The talks were clearly to be more than an exchange of courtesies, for Vansittart,* Hoare's permanent under-secretary, was to be present for them. Even so, they caused Baldwin no particular concern, despite a half-warning from Anthony Eden, who was then a second Cabinet minister in the Foreign Office. A combination of holiday habits and of the location of the League in Geneva meant that staging visits to the Quai d'Orsay by British ministers were part of the normal diplomatic pattern of the twenties and thirties. In any event Baldwin believed in leaving foreign affairs to the Foreign Secretary. He satisfied himself with a few words of hurried consultation during a House of Commons debate. Hoare left for Paris on Friday, 6 December, neither authorized to negotiate nor told not to.

During the next two days the Hoare-Laval Pact was concocted. There was only a French text of the document, but it was initialled by the two ministers, and therefore involved a substantial degree of commitment on both their parts. In effect it provided for the dismemberment of Abyssinia and the giving to Mussolini of about half of what he had set himself to achieve by conquest. It leaked into the French press by the morning of Monday, 9 December.

Hoare's behaviour after concluding the agreement was very strange. He telephoned a Sunday request to London for a Monday Cabinet, sent the proposals back overnight by a Foreign Office official, and left for Switzerland. When Eden, at Baldwin's request, had telephoned him in Paris on the Sunday evening, he was resting and was pronounced unavailable. Vansittart was equally unavailable, but they joined in sending a message that they were both 'well satisfied with the day's work'. With that Baldwin had to be content until almost the Monday noon. It was in a sense the just reward of his method of conducting foreign policy. Ten years earlier a cartoon by David Low* had depicted him as rejecting an appeal for advice by Austen Chamberlain (soon to reappear on the stage of Baldwin's life) and saying, 'But *you* are Foreign Secretary.' Now another Foreign Secretary, much junior, much more Baldwin's protegé, whether through intention or exhaustion, was acting on this precept with avidity.

Baldwin was uneasy about the reaction to the so-called pact, and became more so as a violent storm of influential criticism burst over his head. The editor of *The Times*, most of the bishops (even Lang* of Canterbury), and the whole of the liberal establishment were horrified at the sell-out. But there is no evidence that Baldwin rejected the agreement on its own merits. At Cabinets on 9, 10 and 11 December he cautiously defended it on the ground that Hoare must have known more than they did, and defended also the continuation of Hoare's holiday, although this by then had become more of a matter of nursing than of recreation, for he had fallen on the ice and broken his nose in two places.

Baldwin had also to defend the pact in the House of Commons on 10 December. It was one of the worst-judged and least successful speeches of his life. No doubt in the circumstances success was impossible. Baldwin ought therefore to have had the self-discipline to mumble through an unmemorable failure. Instead he was led astray by the recollection of past triumphs. He raised the stakes when he could not win. He tried to repeat one of his dramatic and opinion-moving orations. 'My lips are not yet unsealed, but if these troubles were over and I could make a full case I guarantee there is not a man that would go into the lobby against us.'[14] It was a ridiculous exaggeration and opinions were not moved. Worse still, 'sealed lips' became one of the political catch-phrases of the thirties. He had imprinted his failure on the public memory.

On 16 December Hoare returned to London, but was not well enough to leave his own house. That evening Baldwin called on him and told him, 'We all stand together.'[15] The next day Neville Chamberlain called and rehearsed with him the defence which Hoare proposed to make to the House of Commons on Thursday, the 19th. At Cabinet on the Wednesday morning the Chancellor reported what the Foreign Secretary (still confined to his house) proposed to say. The members of the Cabinet said they would not have it. If Hoare did not resign, they would. Halifax, Baldwin's most trusted colleague, delivered the *coup de grace*. The moral standing of the Government, he argued, was on trial before the world. If Hoare did not go, the Prime Minister would lose his personal position and 'one of our national anchors would have dragged'.[16]

This was decisive for Baldwin. He would sacrifice many things for a friend, but not his public reputation. He said little more to the Cabinet than that 'it was a worse situation in the House of Commons than he had ever known', but he got Chamberlain (a great man for doing the dirty jobs) to see Hoare again and present him with an impossible ultimatum. Either he abandoned his defence of his own conduct in favour of a complete recantation, or he had to go. When Hoare had decided on resignation, Baldwin himself (accompanied by Eden) went to see him and amiably asked him how he felt. 'I wish I were dead,' was Hoare's discouraging response.[17]

Even with the resignation in his pocket, Baldwin was still facing a nasty prospect in the House of Commons. The Labour Party had put down a vote of censure and there was much rumbling on the Tory backbenches. Austen Chamberlain, it was thought, might lead a substantial group into the lobby against the Government. Baldwin saw Chamberlain and said, 'Austen, when Sam has gone I shall want to talk to you about the Foreign Office.'[18] Chamberlain, at seventy-two, could still be excited by the hint of a return to his old department. Once again, in Birkenhead's phrase, he played the game, and once again he lost it. In the House the following day he seized on the

excuse that Attlee had impugned the Prime Minister's honour*
and called off his revolt. Then Baldwin saw him again and told
him that were it not for his age and his health (neither of which
had greatly changed in the preceding forty-eight hours), he
would have offered him the vacancy, but as it was it had better
go to Eden. Chamberlain, Baldwin suggested, might consider
joining as a minister without portfolio.

Austen Chamberlain not merely declined, but did not subsequently forgive Baldwin. Ten days later he wrote to his sister
saying that he had been asked to write an essay about Baldwin,
but that he had refused, for he wished neither to lie nor to
publish the truth, which he then proceeded to outline:

> And we know him as self-centred, selfish and idle, yet
> one of the shrewdest politicians, but without a con-
> structive idea in his head and with an amazing ignor-
> ancē of Indian and foreign affairs and of the real values
> of political life. 'Sly, Sir, devilishly sly!' would be my
> chapter heading, and egotism and idleness the principal
> characteristics that I should assign to him.[19]

When Chamberlain died, fifteen months later, Baldwin
delivered one of the finest examples of his House of Commons
éloge style. Characteristically he was reminded by the life of the
old politician, product of Edgbaston, long-term resident of
South Kensington, of the rhythms of the English countryside.
With a still greater capacity for self-deception, he assured the
House that Austen Chamberlain never had an unkind thought
about any man.

The scars of the Hoare-Laval fiasco remained visible on

---

* It is very difficult for opposition leaders to strike the right note to entice Government supporters. Twenty years later, at the time of Suez, Gaitskell was held to have
minimized the Conservative revolt, not by impugning Eden's honour, but by offering
too direct an appeal to the dissidents. The best parliamentary course, when Government revolts are simmering, might be for opposition spokesmen to say nothing, but
that would hardly be compatible with their position in the country, or with their
providing a lobby into which the dissidents might be enticed. The reality often is that
those who have threatened to revolt are looking with considerable eagerness for an
excuse to change their minds.

Baldwin for most of the next year. The incident, and his own weak, almost contemptible handling of it came near to making his third premiership seem to himself and others an ill-judged prolongation of power, a disastrous epilogue to the rest of his career. Throughout the remainder of the 1935–6 session he was exhausted, depressed and bereft of any reserve of prestige. Jones found him 'very low' in February. That same month, bowing to pressure, he agreed to appoint a Minister for the Coordination of Defence. Guilty, and with some cause, he wanted to bring Hoare back, but was persuaded it was too soon.* When he was then slow in announcing a name, Churchill enjoyed himself with the *mot* that 'Baldwin has to find a man of inferior ability to himself, and this Herculean task requires time for its accomplishment.' Eventually the appointment of the Attorney-General (Thomas Inskip*) was announced and received with a mixture of ridicule and dismay.

That spring Baldwin became manifestly deafer. He often could not hear questions in the House of Commons and had to have them repeated to him by Margesson,* his Chief Whip. When he made a successful speech to the Conservative back-bench committee it was a matter of surprised comment. His most popular decision of 1936 was to fix the date of his own retirement, which was to be in May 1937.

In June, with eleven months still to go, he was told by his doctor that his state of nervous exhaustion was such that if he did not immediately take a week's rest at Chequers (which with Parliament sitting inevitably involved a public announcement) he would not survive without collapse until the end of July. During this enforced week, even the faithful and normally encouraging Davidson wrote to tell him that 'Every mongrel is yapping, believing that a very tired fox has gone to ground at Chequers, with no fight left in him.'[20] He got back for July, but only to complain of 'the day-to-day badgering' to which he was subjected in the House of Commons. It sounded more like

---

* Hoare came back in June as First Lord of the Admiralty.

MacDonald than the old parliamentary master. He was pressed to reduce the size of the Cabinet, but hopelessly excused himself to Jones: 'I have told Neville he may be able to do something. I cannot . . . I am too tired for any fresh effort.'[21]

At the beginning of August he left for a two and a half months' rest at sequestered Welsh and English houses.* He was too exhausted even to go to Aix. His one piece of good fortune that summer was that he resisted (for the second time) strong pressure from Jones for a meeting with Hitler. Lethargy had its advantages. His premiership appeared not so much to be running out as running down. Few believed that when he came back in the autumn he would be able to do more than coast gently and desultorily along for another six months. As it happened, the reality turned out to be quite different. There was a last turn-up for Baldwin's book.

---

* He went first to Gregynog, the Montgomeryshire house of the Davies family (see note on Tom Jones, *infra*), and then to Blickling, the Norfolk house of the 11th Marquess of Lothian (1882–1940), formerly as Philip Kerr a member of Milner's South African 'Kindergarten' and then of Lloyd George's 'garden suburb' secretariat, currently a close associate of Waldorf (2nd Viscount) and Nancy Astor, and hence a core member of the 'Cliveden Set'. When he died at the end of 1940 (perhaps because Nancy Astor had converted him from Roman Catholicism to Christian Science and turned him against doctors) he was British Ambassador in Washington.

CHAPTER SEVEN

Abdication and Retirement

King George V died on 20 January 1936. Although the quiet-
ness of his end was made memorable by Reith's BBC
announcement that 'the King's life is moving peacefully
towards its close', there had been no long-term illness during
which an early change of reign had been accepted and prepared
for. The King was only just over seventy, and he had been well
enough to make one of his 'bluff Englishman's' jokes about the
Hoare *débâcle*,* to spend his usual Christmas and New Year in
the Norfolk countryside, and to deliver his Christmas broadcast
from there. He did not see Baldwin after he became ill,
although he held a Privy Council on the morning of the day of
his death.

Had the pattern of the King's demise been different, so too
might have been the whole shape of the end of Baldwin's
premiership. It is now clear that the King had the gravest
doubts about the general suitability of his heir for the Throne,
and that these doubts went far enough to turn his mind
towards the desirability of getting his second son to succeed
instead. His thoughts were matched by those of Baldwin and of
the other senior ministers. From the beginning they had a solid
lack of confidence in King Edward VIII. 'S.B. is distinctly
nervous about him,' Jones recorded on the first day of the new
reign.[1] And at the Accession Council that same afternoon,
Baldwin told Attlee, to whom he was not close, that he doubted

---

* 'You know what they are saying,' Anthony Eden reported that he had said. 'No
more coals to Newcastle, no more Hoares to Paris' (Eden, *Facing the Dictators*, p. 317).
Kenneth Rose's *King George V* casts doubt on the authenticity of this remark.

whether the King would 'stay the course'. It was not merely Mrs Simpson, although ministers were already well-informed about his relationship with her, if not his marital intentions. It was his general attitude of irresponsibility, selfishness, and dislike for any of the functions of kingship other than easy popularity and personal privilege. Nor were these feelings of unease confined to Baldwin. Neville Chamberlain, always more censorious and more practical, produced a detailed memorandum, early in the reign, suggesting that the Government should submit to the new King a general programme for the improvement of tone, including the wearing of darker suits.

A meeting of minds between the old King and his Prime Minister (fortified by the support of Chamberlain, Baldwin's clear successor) might not therefore have been difficult to achieve. But it would have required a conversation between them in circumstances when the subject of an imminent new reign could naturally have been discussed. And a remaining obstacle to firm dealing with the Prince of Wales would have been Baldwin's deep-rooted distaste for grasping nettles which were not pushed into his hands. Perhaps it would have been necessary, in order to eliminate the reign of King Edward VIII, not merely for King George V to have lived a few months under the sentence of death, but for Neville Chamberlain, never one for tolerant inactivity whatever his other faults, to have succeeded MacDonald in 1935. Neither of these events occurred. Baldwin was therefore left reluctantly with the responsibility, in his own words, 'of having to take charge of the Prince as King'.[2] This was a substantial cause of his low spirits during much of 1936. He thought there was trouble ahead, but he was disinclined to do anything about it before he had to. He noted gloomily that when he dined with the King in May the Simpsons were both present, and that when another semi-political dinner party was given in July Mrs Simpson was announced in the Court Circular as being present alone without her husband. The movement was unfavourable but the position not yet critical.

This changed when Baldwin came back to London in October. What had previously been gossip only within a small circle had become widely known throughout the world, excepting however that substantial part of the British public which did not have international contacts. The British press continued to display a discretion which was a remarkable tribute to the influence of the Palace as an institution with the 'respectable' proprietors, and of the King himself with Rothermere and Beaverbrook. Neither the American nor most of the European press was subject to such restraints, and their readers had been regaled throughout the summer with photographs and titillating reports of a royal cruise down the Dalmatian coast. This produced a flood of letters to Downing Street, which were kept from Baldwin during his long holiday, but which hit him with the force of a tidal wave on his return. At the same time there was the dread news that a Simpson divorce case had been set down for hearing at Ipswich, chosen because it could there be more easily hurried on, for 27 October. King Edward VIII was clearly moving outside the waters which had been well charted by King Edward VII. The last thing that Mrs Keppel would have been encouraged to do was to get a divorce.

The prospect was intimidating. Today, over fifty years after the beginning of the testing but successful reign of King George VI, the Abdication looks merely an unusual transition from one sovereign to another. Before it took place, it seemed almost equally likely that the premature end of King Edward's reign might result, not in the succession of his brother, but in the collapse of the monarchy. Nevertheless, Baldwin's reaction to the new developments was not wholly one of dismay.

He had had his rest, his metabolism responded well to an occasional crisis, he had long known there was one looming here, and he may have sensed that there were advantages, both public and private, in bringing it to a head before the end of his premiership. Furthermore, it gave him an excellent excuse not to apply his mind to the dismal subjects – rearmament, the war in Spain, relations with Hitler, the distressed areas – the weight of which had built up during his absence. The Abdication was an issue where British public opinion, not intransigent foreigners or intractable facts, was likely to be decisive, and one on which, therefore, his old gifts of timing, mood creation, and putting an adversary in the wrong, should be of pre-eminent value. The first minister he saw after taking in the new facts was Eden, in many ways his favourite at the time. With suppressed excitement and relief at the possibility of preoccupation, he told the Foreign Secretary that the crisis of the monarchy was upon them, that he (Eden) must go and read his own overseas correspondence on the subject (which he had not apparently hitherto done), and that he must not trouble him (Baldwin) too much with foreign affairs just now. Eden wrote: 'After three months without a comment from the Prime Minister' (he had not seen him during this period, which included the 'internationalization' of the Spanish Civil War), 'I found this an astonishing doctrine.'[3]

At the end of his first week back, Baldwin went to stay at Cumberland Lodge, in Windsor Great Park, only a few miles from Fort Belvedere, a *bijou* residence which justified its martial name only by looking like a toy castle, but which was nonetheless the King's main base throughout his brief reign. The proximity did not however imply that the Prime Minister was moving amongst the King's friends. The host was Lord FitzAlan,* a Roman Catholic and a former Chief Whip. The guests he had assembled to meet the Prime Minister included Lord Salisbury, Anglican and hereditary bearer of the conscience of the Conservative peers, Lord Kemsley, Welsh and nonconformist by origin, portentous press lord by achievement, and the Duke of Norfolk, leading Catholic layman, nephew of FitzAlan, and responsible as Earl Marshal for the organization of the Coronation – if it took place. In addition, Alexander Hardinge,* who had replaced Wigram as private secretary to the King and who constantly saw his loyalty as lying with the institution and not with the person, was available to come over at short notice and did so. The King hardly needed to have a net laid for him, but had he done so it would have been difficult to assemble, almost in his own backyard, a more obvious team of trappers.

Those assembled were unanimous that the King could not be allowed to proceed as he was doing. But the main practical outcome of the weekend was to brace Baldwin, in favourable surroundings, for a first confrontation. This took place at Fort Belvedere at 10.30 on the morning of the following Tuesday, 20 October. The King was brought back from Sandringham. Baldwin drove across from Chequers. It was hardly a convenient location for either. But at least it was a most beautiful morning and St Luke's Day, the heart of the Indian summer, as Baldwin noted. He complimented the King upon his herbaceous borders, but otherwise was uneasy. After a short time he asked if he could have a whisky and soda, and when the ingredients were brought tried to pour a drink for the King. 'Sir, when?' he oddly and unwisely said. It was too easy a trick to miss. The King assured Baldwin that he never drank before seven in the evening and settled down to listen to the lecture that he knew was coming. Baldwin started in a circumlocutory way, but he appears eventually to have been fairly blunt. 'I don't believe you can go on like this and get away with it,' was his core phrase, prepared with care because he believed that it was in the King's idiom. He asked for the divorce to be put off, which the King said was Mrs Simpson's business, and he urged that she should go away for six months. He omitted to ask whether the King intended to marry her after the divorce, but this apart he discharged his difficult duty faithfully.

He did not at this stage bring the matter before the whole Cabinet, but confined himself to informing four or five senior ministers of what had occurred. Nor did he do much else about it. He consulted a few people whom he thought were good tests of opinion. He tried (unsuccessfully) to get Mackenzie King, who was visiting, to speak as bluntly to the King as he had done himself, but the Canadian Prime Minister, although agreeing with Baldwin, preferred to use his audience for flattery rather than warning. From mid-October to mid-November Baldwin behaved as though he still hoped that the King might retreat and the affair blow over. Probably he did not think this likely to happen. Possibly he did not want it to happen. But he thought there was advantage in giving it an opportunity to do so.

Neville Chamberlain thought otherwise. He encouraged Sir Warren Fisher, the permanent secretary of the Treasury, and other senior civil servants to busy themselves with the drawing up of constitutional memoranda which came near to being ultimata. Their tone is indicated by Chamberlain's draft of a 'friendly' precursor of a formal submission for Baldwin to send to the King:

> I have before me an official communication in which the advice of Your Majesty's Government is formally tendered, to the effect that in view of the grave danger to which, in their opinion, this country is being exposed, your association with Mrs Simpson should be terminated forthwith. It is hardly necessary for me to point out that should this advice be tendered and refused by Your Majesty, only one result could follow in accordance with the requirements of constitutional monarchy, that is, the resignation of myself and the National Government. If Mrs Simpson left the country forthwith, this distasteful matter could be settled in a less formal manner.[4]

Chamberlain obviously thought the King should be dealt with more like the Poplar Board of Guardians than like Hitler. Baldwin was horrified by these draft documents. They offended his sense of emollience and he also realized that, if submitted and published, their clamant discourtesy would almost certainly have the effect of swinging opinion towards the King. He took the documents away and metaphorically buried them, but not before they had made him realize that he could not allow the matter to drift for much longer.

The same realization came to the King, pushed towards his

precipice by Hardinge harshly telling him that he could not go on without a decision. A second meeting between Sovereign and Prime Minister (on the King's initiative) took place on 16 November.* At this meeting the question of marriage was raised (there is a conflict of evidence as to by whom). The King asked whether it would be approved, and Baldwin skilfully replied that it would not be acceptable to the country, thereby keeping any question of the Government's own veto in the background. The King then said he would abdicate in order to marry. According to his account to the House of Commons, Baldwin replied: 'Sir, that is most grievous news, and it is impossible for me to make any comment on it today.' According to Mrs Baldwin, whose account was more immediate, the words were: 'Sir, this is a very grave decision and I am deeply grieved'; but the significant difference is that she adds: 'and he went on to tell him that according to some legal opinion the divorce ought not to have been granted, that there were certain aspects of it that in any ordinary case would not have gone through.' This was perhaps the one element of veiled blackmail in Baldwin's dealing with the King, the faint suggestion that if he was too awkward with the Government he might end up without either the Throne or the freedom to marry Mrs Simpson.†

Between then and the next meeting on 25 November the idea of a morganatic marriage was put into the minds of both the King and Baldwin. The King was attracted, Baldwin was not. The King pressed for formal consideration, to which Baldwin agreed, although pointing out that this would involve both the Cabinet and the Dominion Prime Ministers. On 27

---

* Even without an unprecedented impending crisis, a month was an unusually long interval between Prime Ministerial audiences.

† The point arose because of the latent powers of a legal luminary known as the King's Proctor. Lady Donaldson's *Edward VIII* contains the following neat explanation: 'As the law stood at the time the fact that two people both wished to divorce each other was an absolute bar to their being able to do so. Thus if it could be proved that the divorce was arranged 'collusively' between the two parties, the application would fail' (page 238). A decree *nisi* could also be set aside on the intervention of the King's Proctor during the period before it became absolute. (See also page 153 *infra*.)

November the Cabinet was accordingly officially informed of the whole matter for the first time. Except perhaps for Duff Cooper, who was the closest to the King, they were all against the morganatic proposal. So, too, were those of the Dominion Prime Ministers who had a view. Lyons of Australia was particularly strong, Mackenzie King and Hertzog of South Africa a shade less so. De Valera was only interested in using the crisis to loosen the links of the Irish Free State with the Crown, and Savage of New Zealand, somewhat surprisingly, veered between unconcern and bewilderment.

Baldwin's object was then to resolve the crisis with reasonable speed without appearing to force the hand of the King. He had audiences on 2 and 4 December. On the first occasion he gave the King the result of the consultations with the Cabinet and the Dominions. That killed the morganatic marriage plan. He then vetoed the King's request to be allowed to make his own appeal to the British people. A King, he said, could only do so in terms approved by his ministers. The King then said: 'You want me to go, don't you?' Baldwin answered with commendable frankness: what he wanted, what he thought the King himself wanted, was for him to go, if he had to, as quietly as possible, and thereby to make things easier for his successor.* On the following evening the King, detecting a hint of impatience in the Prime Minister, said with some bitterness: 'You will not have to wait much longer, Mr Baldwin.'

Both King and Prime Minister were becoming a little strained. Baldwin was being buffeted from several sides. An arrow shot almost accidentally by the Bishop of Bradford had given the press an excuse to break their self-imposed conspiracy of silence and bring the whole matter into the public domain. A substantial part of the Cabinet was pressing for a quick outcome. The Chancellor of the Exchequer showed that the traditions of 'Brummagen' radical commercialism had not died with his father by being most worried about the effect of

* The King might perhaps at this point have paraphrased Baldwin's own remark about successors to Neville Chamberlain six years earlier (see page 118 *supra*).

continued uncertainty upon the Christmas trade. The opposition were loyally supporting the Government, but were also pressing for a definitive statement. Churchill, on the other hand, with the support of the *Daily Mail*, the *Daily Express* and, more surprisingly, the *News Chronicle*, was feeling his way towards a King's Party. In the House of Commons on the afternoon of Thursday, 3 December, he got a sizeable cheer when he spoke against any 'irrevocable step'.

Baldwin rightly thought that this particular bubble would be pricked over the weekend. MPs would be steadied against the King by their constituents.* By the Monday they were to shout down with peculiar virulence a similar although more long-winded question by Churchill. Nevertheless, Baldwin felt his time was running short. This led him to make his one dangerous error of the whole affair. A possible intervention of the King's Proctor to upset the divorce had for some time been lurking in the Government's mind. It was of course the point of Baldwin's remark to the King on 16 November. The Attorney-General had, under instructions, done a good deal of work on the issue. The Government had played with it as a possible weapon against the King. Now it was suddenly turned against them. The advice was that the Proctor could not act against his nominal royal master. But once the King had abdicated he would cease to have this protection. Walter Monckton,• his legal adviser, seized the point, and on Saturday, 5 December, asked almost as a condition of Abdication, that a special bill should be introduced to make the decree immediately absolute, and thus remove the danger.

That evening, in his small black police car, Baldwin trundled again down the new arterial road through the western suburbs for another uneasy interview at Fort Belvedere. Baldwin agreed that the request for a special bill was reasonable and said that he would commend it to his colleagues. Next day in

* It was not that he had an inflated view of the assiduity of their consultations. 'But how they do it I don't know,' he told G. M. Young. 'I suppose they talk to the stationmaster' (Young, *Stanley Baldwin*, page 242).

Downing Street he ran into solid opposition. The arguments against putting through Parliament a blatant twisting of the general law, which would smell only too strongly of a corrupt bargain, were overwhelming. Probably Baldwin saw their force himself. Certainly he did not fight very hard. But his authority within the Government slipped momentarily, and worse still, there was a danger that the whole Abdication timetable might be upset. Monckton, when brought into the meeting of ministers (it was not a full Cabinet) to be told of the adverse decision, said that it might delay matters by weeks. Fortunately for Baldwin, Monckton misjudged his client. The King had settled himself into such a groove of petulant determination that there was no question of the rejection of the bargain deflecting him for even a few days. He was equally uninfluenced by a curious offer of withdrawal which Mrs Simpson made from Cannes on the Monday.

Tuesday was the last day of uncertainty. In one sense Baldwin felt much more confident. Monday afternoon in the House of Commons had been as great a triumph for him (although he had said practically nothing) as it had been a disaster for Churchill. 'The stationmasters' had clearly done their work. Henceforward he could be assured that a King's Party would get nowhere in Parliament. But he was worried about the King's mental state, and to what this might lead. He decided to deal with the problem in a way which imported a substantial element of farce into the overcharged atmosphere, although his object was not to provide light relief. The King, he decided, 'must wrestle with himself in a way he has never done before, and if he will let me, I will help him. We may even have to see the night through together.'[5] Accordingly Baldwin packed his suitcase, instructed his parliamentary private secretary to do the same, and set off yet once more in the small black car. When the King saw the luggage being unloaded he was horrified. It was tactfully conveyed to Baldwin that he would be welcome to stay for dinner but not afterwards. His attempt at a soul-searching vigil had been frustrated. It was in any event unnecessary. The King seemed decided, friendly and even buoyant. There was no bitterness between them at this stage. If that came, it came later, when the King had time to go over events and perhaps have his grievances kindled. When, late that night, they parted for the last time, Baldwin's words were a little rehearsed,* but there nonetheless appears to have been genuine emotion on both sides.

Yet the question remains as to what Baldwin thought he might have attempted in a long night of 'reasoning together'. G. M. Young is explicit. He tells us that Baldwin later told a friend: 'Only time I was frightened. I thought he might change his mind.'[6] Unfortunately the friend is anonymous, and Young, that strangely and personally chosen official biographer, cannot always be regarded as a witness either of truth or charity. But on this occasion the weight of reason is decisively on his side. Surely Baldwin, whatever his desire earlier in the imbroglio, cannot at this stage have wished to go back to the Cabinet on the following morning and announce that a wayward King, who had already compromised his position with most opinion both at home and in the Dominions, had suddenly changed his mind, at least temporarily, and, having attracted the maximum publicity to his preference for Mrs Simpson over the Throne, was now prepared to ditch her and try to pick up again the pieces of kingship. This for Baldwin would surely have been the worst of both worlds. Yet it was precisely what the Cabinet went through the motions of trying to achieve at its meeting that next (Wednesday) morning. It sent through Baldwin a submission to the King of which the key paragraph read:

Ministers are reluctant to believe that Your Majesty's resolve is irrevocable and still venture to hope that

* The King's account is that he said: 'I know that you and Mrs Baldwin do not approve of what I am doing, but I belong to a different generation;' and that Baldwin replied: 'Sir, it is quite true that there are no two people amongst your subjects who are more grieved at what has happened than we are, but you must always remember that there are no two people who hope more sincerely that you may find happiness where you believe it to be found' (A King's Story, page 402).

before Your Majesty pronounces any formal decision
Your Majesty may be pleased to reconsider an intention
which must so deeply and so vitally affect all Your
Majesty's subjects.[7]

Within a few minutes of receiving this the King had written
back regretting that he was unable to alter his decision. It is
difficult to believe that the submission, valuable for the record
and indeed used by Baldwin in his House of Commons speech
the following afternoon, would have been sent had Baldwin
not satisfied himself the night before what the answer would
be. This was, indeed, little more than common prudence.

On the Thursday (10 December) Baldwin presented the King's
message of renunciation to the House of Commons, and followed it by his own account and justification of events. It was a
remarkable speech on at least three counts. First, major constitutional and political pronouncement though it was, certain to
be studied and analysed for years to come, he delivered it with
hardly a note. He had made some, but he first left them behind
in Downing Street, and then, when they had been retrieved,
allowed them to rest, unreferred to, on the despatch box. What
he gave was a chronological narrative, apparently searching his
memory as he went along. At one stage he turned to the Home
Secretary, sitting beside him, and said: 'It was that day, was it
not?' Art and nature were most skilfully intertwined.

Second, he navigated his way through complicated channels
and delicate shoals without any jarring note. Nearly everyone –
except Mrs Simpson – got a tribute. They all appeared to be
appropriately and spontaneously phrased. No foot was put
wrong. Third, the effect upon the House was profound. When,
towards the end, he said, 'I am convinced that where I have
failed no one could have succeeded,' this appeared not a boast,
but an understatement. When he sat down it was almost
impossible to continue even a *pro forma* debate. Attlee wisely
suggested a ninety-minute adjournment before attempting
to do so. Baldwin was aware – as emerged from a corridor

encounter with Harold Nicolson● during this adjournment[8] –
of how great had been his triumph. He was probably also aware
that it was to be his last on any comparable scale.

The speech lasted exactly forty-five minutes, which, particularly as Baldwin spoke slowly, was not long. The language was
not majestic, nor the order wholly logical. But the effect was
almost magical. The contrast between Baldwin's deflation at
the end of 1935 and his prestige at the end of 1936 was as sharp
as can possibly be imagined. He was again exhausted. Lord
Dawson of Penn, that specialist in the industrial diseases of
politicians, joined in the general chorus of congratulation but
also told him, speaking medically and not politically: 'You will
pay for this.' But he did not do so immediately. He had a good
Christmas. 'We had a wonderful day yesterday . . . ,' he wrote
to Tom Jones on Boxing Day. 'The sunrise was as the opening
of the gates of heaven itself and the glow it threw on the
western hills transfigured the whole landscape for half an hour.
The strange unearthly light lasted nearly all day.'[9]

What precisely was Baldwin's achievement in the handling
of the Abdication? It was perhaps best summed up by Sir
Donald Somervell,● the Attorney-General, who was closely yet
not responsibly involved throughout, and who was therefore
an informed and detached witness:

Baldwin [he wrote] was the man who enabled the crisis
to be surmounted with the minimum of discredit. He
decided, and finally decided, the following as soon as
they appeared for decision:
(1) That Mrs Simpson could never be Queen.
(2) That the King would not give up the chance of
marrying Mrs Simpson.
(3) That a morganatic marriage was impracticable.
(4) That the decision must be the King's own decision.
He may have realised earlier than most of us that
the King was in the long run unfitted to be King. If
so it is all the greater tribute to his qualities that he

never took a step to force the issue or to encourage abdication.[10]

This is a fair tribute. MacDonald, had he still been Prime Minister, would have lost the issue in verbiage and drowned himself in self-pity. Neville Chamberlain, had he already succeeded, would have alienated the country by treating the King like a negligent Town Clerk of Birmingham. Attlee, had he won the 1935 election, would have taken exactly Baldwin's line in substance, but at that stage in his career would have done so without assurance or persuasiveness. Churchill, had he by chance been already in power, would simply have been wrong.

This last comparison provokes one further reflection. In the three and a half years between his abdication and the summer of Dunkirk, King Edward, had he remained on the Throne, might have developed differently. He might have shed his Lindbergh-like naiveté and enthusiasm for simple solutions which made him an easy prey to authoritarianism and the meretricious appeal of Nazis and fascists. He might, but equally he might not. And had the latter been the case, Churchill, almost his only substantial political ally of 1936, would in 1940 have been confronted with a very awkward decision as to whether to intern his sovereign. It would, to say the least, have added a further complication to the problems of 1940. Britain was almost alone amongst European states in surviving the convulsions of 1939–45 without a change of regime. Two Americans made substantial contributions to this continuity. The first, obviously, was President Roosevelt. The second, inadvertently, was Mrs Simpson.

In the midst of his Abdication preoccupations Baldwin made one major speech on another subject. This was on 12 November, in the debate on the Address at the opening of the new session. Rearmament was the dominant issue, at least within the Conservative Party. Immediately before the summer recess, and as one of his last acts before his two and a half months of asylum, Baldwin had devoted two days to receiving an almost unprecedented deputation on the subject. Austen Chamberlain and Salisbury were the nominal leaders, but Churchill was the moving spirit, and delivered a prepared private oration lasting over an hour. There were fifteen or so others present, many of them Privy Councillors, all of considerable party or national weight. Baldwin, supported by Sir Thomas Inskip, listened during three- or four-hour sessions on each of the successive days. He said little, as might have been expected, although one of his *obiter dicta* is remarkable both for its potential value, had it been publicly known, to the Soviet apologists of 1939–40, and for the slovenliness, almost the vulgarity, of language for the occasion. 'I am not going to get this country into a war with anybody for the League of Nations or anybody else or for anything else,' Baldwin is recorded as saying. 'If there is any fighting in Europe, I should like to see the Bolshies and the Nazis doing it.'[11]

Against this background Baldwin in November felt under some pressure from his backbenches, particularly as his speech had been preceded by a denunciation, at once contrived and powerful, from Churchill. Baldwin's reply was not very different from words he had used to the July deputation, but this time of course he was speaking in public and with his words immediately available for all to refer to:

> I put before the whole House my own views with an appalling frankness [he typically but unwisely began the crucial passage]. From 1933, I and my friends were all very worried about what was happening in Europe. . . . You will remember at that time there was probably a stronger pacifist feeling running through the country than at any time since the War. I am speaking of 1933 and 1934. You will remember the election at Fulham in the autumn of 1933, when a seat which the National Government held was lost by about 7,000 votes on no issue but the pacifist. . . .
>
> That was the feeling in the country in 1933. My

position as a leader of a great party was not altogether a comfortable one. I asked myself what chance was there ... within the next year or two of that feeling being so changed that the country would give a mandate for rearmament? Supposing I had gone to the country and said that Germany was rearming and we must rearm, does anybody think that this pacific democracy would have rallied to that cry at that moment? I cannot think of anything that would have made the loss of the election from my point of view more certain.[12]

There was no great immediate excitement, but the passage, and particularly the last sentence, reverberated against Baldwin for many years to come. It led Churchill, twelve years later, when Baldwin had just died, to publish, in the first volume of his *Second World War*, one of the most polemical and therefore famous of all footnote references. 'Baldwin, Stanley, confesses to putting party before country, p. 615,' it ran. G. M. Young did not contest this judgment, which has led subsequent biographers* to attempt elaborate textual exegesis in order to show that Baldwin's remarks were venial because he was referring to a hypothetical election in 1933 or 1934, and not to the actual one in 1935. By then he was prepared to advocate rearmament.

The year 1937 was an easy and agreeable one for Baldwin. His energy and his power were still running out. But, thanks to his handling of the Abdication, a glow of achievement had replaced the murk of anti-climax which seemed likely, during most of 1936, to surround his final period of office. He was able to plan with precision and enthusiasm the date of his own retirement, to look forward to it because it was in no way forced upon him, and to believe that he would be remembered with affection and regret. He was the only Prime Minister between Lord Salisbury (who resigned in 1902) and Harold Wilson (in 1976) to make such an unforced departure. And Salisbury,

* Middlemas and Barnes, 1969, and Montgomery Hyde, 1973.

who died in 1903, was unlike Baldwin in not having the opportunity of enjoying his repose.

During the final months Baldwin handed over more and more power to Neville Chamberlain. After the changeover he soon and predictably became critical of Chamberlain, but before it took place he seemed wholly unattracted by the game of balancing one possible successor against another. Chamberlain was not everyone's favourite, even within his own party. He made a bad Budget error* on the threshold of the succession, many Tory MPs were said to prefer (of all people) Inskip, and there seems no doubt that Baldwin, had he wished, could have stirred up a good cauldron of uncertainty. He did not so wish. Perhaps, despite lack of affection, he felt he owed Chamberlain something after so many years of efficient subordination. Perhaps he feared that any doubt would mean the postponement of his own release. And, lassitude apart, he had more than enough sense to see that after the triumph of the Abdication, with the memory of the vicissitudes of the previous year so fresh in his mind, a calm movement away from the gaming tables and towards the chip-cashing *caisse* was obviously prudent.

May 28 1937, sixteen days after the Coronation of King George VI, became the chosen date. His last speech in the House was more than three weeks before, and the occasion seemed to be organized by all concerned as a commemorative epitome. There was a threatened dispute at a Yorkshire colliery. As there was a London bus strike actually taking place this threat, even if it materialized, seemed fairly peripheral to the success or otherwise of the Coronation. Nevertheless it was brought before the House, Baldwin came down, spoke movingly of 'our young King and Queen' who were about to 'dedicate themselves to the service of their people', and pulled out, gently and without tension, all his old stops about industrial peace, democracy and the avoidance of strife. Tom

---

* By announcing a National Defence Contribution which was a tax not on profits as such but on their increase. He united Keynes and Montagu Norman against him. His proposal was withdrawn on the day he kissed hands.

Williams,* Labour Member for the constituency in which the colliery was situated, announced that it would be folly to continue the debate, and the dispute, perhaps not a very difficult one in any event, got itself settled. The old maestro having been asked to give a last exhibition of his art, no one wished it to go wrong.

His final Cabinet was on 26 May. Chamberlain paid a tribute to Baldwin, which while predictably pedestrian, was a great deal less embarrassing than Harcourt's reading from 'a well-thumbed manuscript' at the famous 'blubbering Cabinet' which said farewell to Gladstone in 1894. Baldwin then paid another tribute to MacDonald (still there as Lord President of the Council), for whom it was also the end. The next day in the House of Commons he was able not only to listen to tributes to himself – a rare experience, normally confined to a man's widow – but to perform the rôle of an out-of-season Father Christmas. He announced an increase in Members' salaries from £400 to £600. It was particularly welcome on the Labour side of the House. He left the Palace of Westminster that afternoon on a wave of fulfilment and popularity. It was most unusual in British politics, as much for its measured orderliness as for its warmth. Changes of Prime Minister normally occur more abruptly and disagreeably. It was, of course, much too good to last.

Baldwin became an earl and a knight of the garter. As happened with Balfour, the second honour, being quicker to confer, came first, and he was briefly and incongruously Sir Stanley Baldwin. Then, ten days later, he became Earl Baldwin of Bewdley. His residential problems were fewer than in 1929. He left Downing Street after three or four days, and Chequers after a fortnight. But so far from there being any question of selling Astley, he was able once again to take a full-scale London house in Eaton Square. The shares of Baldwins Ltd had made a substantial recovery. His annual income, including his Prime Minister's pension of £2000, was between £15,000 and £20,000 (the equivalent of £300/400,000 today).

Almost the only incident to mar the near perfection of the period immediately surrounding his retirement was the absence of any reply to a somewhat sententious letter of reminiscence and good wishes which he sent to the Duke of Windsor (as King Edward had become). Perhaps the Duke (his temper not improved by his wife having just been refused the style of HRH) thought that Baldwin had already done well enough out of the events six months before, without an entitlement to further expressions of fulsome goodwill.

Soon, and no doubt inevitably, some more substantial specks of cloud began to appear in the sky. In July there was a return of the nervous trouble of the previous year. He could not stay in London until the end of the session as he had intended to do. Then in August the Aix visit went wrong. His arthritis made it impossible for him to walk as he had been used to doing. As a result he became bored and left early. So often he had struggled to stay on when others were trying to get him back. It was a typical paradox that now, when he could, had he wished, have stayed for the whole autumn, he should leave before the allotted time was up.*

During that autumn (of 1937) he attended a few more commemorative occasions but made no political speeches. There was at first little to engage his political interest, but this changed after Eden's resignation in February 1938. He liked Eden, and he found it easy to disapprove of the way in which Chamberlain had handled relations with him. He saw a good deal of Eden in the next months, and with a genuine desire to see him Prime Minister gave him a lot of advice. Unfortunately most of it was wrong. He could be shrewd in analysis, as when he told Eden that if war came 'the country will want [Churchill] to lead them', but that Eden's chances were better in peace.[13]

He was less strong on recipes for action. He advised Eden to

* Despite this anti-climax the Baldwins went back to Aix in the summer of 1938 for what turned out to be the last of seventeen visits. They also spent a month at the old Riviera resort of Beaulieu in each of the two last winters of peacetime.

stay away from the House of Commons and to make some non-political speeches in the country on subjects such as 'England'. He became increasingly willing to see him wound Chamberlain, but had no idea how a resigned minister should conduct an attacking campaign. His own experience – always, except once, resisting and not provoking the attacks – had been so different. His other trouble was that he did not really agree with Eden on policy. He was as much of an appeaser as Chamberlain, but less dogmatic and self-righteous. He was looking not for a new policy for Britain, but for a political protegé for himself, someone who would be more gracious and romantic than Chamberlain. But he was not himself able to be of much help. He had no great store of political influence, and he never made any effective use of the platform of the House of Lords. He spoke there only very infrequently, and then tentatively and ineffectively. His post-Munich speech was a typical example. He would not have gone to Munich himself, he said, but he praised Chamberlain's courage for acting differently. The chance of peace must be clung to, but the time gained must be used well. He concealed his real criticism, which was that the 'Peace with Honour' statement was a piece of emotional exhibitionism, and as a result his speech lacked any real impact. The old master of the House of Commons, despite his quiet style, never found his feet in the House of Lords.

Even so, the last two years of peace were for Baldwin a time of interest, enjoyment and even influence, compared with what was to come afterwards. As late as the summer of 1939 Sir Stafford Cripps, expelled from the Labour Party and hardly a natural Baldwin man, was urging him to be a brick in a wall of anti-appeasement national unity. Baldwin was also still in strong demand, at home and abroad, as a deliverer of lectures and addresses of note and distinction. In both April and August 1939 he was in North America, his first visit to Canada since the Ottawa Conference of 1932, his first visit to the United States since his debt negotiation of 1923. From the second visit he returned to an England on the verge of war. He never lived in

Eaton Square again. Astley was half taken over by evacuees. Worse, and more important, it was an England in which he first ceased to have a rôle, and then a year or so later acquired a minor and disagreeable one.

In the winter of 1939–40 he became still more critical of Chamberlain. In May 1940, he believed that his replacement by Churchill was wholly desirable. He was not seduced, although his excuse for this would have been much better than most, by the politically widespread enthusiasm for the alternative of his old friend Halifax. Later in 1940, when Chamberlain was dying, Baldwin wrote him a notable letter of sympathy and warmth. 'Whatever S.B. cannot do,' Tom Jones had written three years earlier, 'he can speak a funeral oration.'[14] He could also write a valedictory letter.

Chamberlain's death left Baldwin more exposed. He became the best available villain for those who wished to fasten upon an individual to blame for Britain's plight. His mail became abusive. His press, when anyone bothered to write about him, became almost uniformly hostile. There was a damaging row about the requisition for scrap of his wrought-iron gates. Some suggested that the whole estate and house ought to be taken over. By the standards of a Blum or a Reynaud he was hardly subjected to persecution. He lived quietly in half his old house, he sometimes went to visit friends in other parts of the country, and occasionally to London, where he stayed in the Dorchester Hotel and was asked to luncheon by Churchill, whose venom was reserved for the index of his book. But he lost nearly all the glow of affection and respect in which he had retired. Most people forgot about him; and the majority of those who did not were unpleasant.

He was again short of money. His material fortunes always seemed to be less stable than those of most rich men. Astley became very run down. By the last year of the war, when he was seventy-seven, he was a rather decrepit old man, living in a rather decrepit old house. He kept up a routine of a sort, but as, from a mixture of laziness and disapproval of political scribblers like Lloyd George and Churchill, he never wrote anything, and increasingly preferred sniffing old books to reading new ones, there was not much purpose to his life. The end of the war, perhaps even the political upheaval of 1945, might have produced a lightening of spirit and a new interest. But Lucy Baldwin died between VE day and the general election. Baldwin was very uxorious and became still more bereft.

He devoted some considerable part of his attention to arranging for G. M. Young, his friend as he thought, to write his biography. It turned out, although of course he never saw it, to be both unfriendly and inadequate. Almost his last public engagement was to go to London in October 1947 and attend the unveiling of the statue of King George V in Old Palace Yard. He was almost unrecognized. Two months later he died in his sleep at Astley. He was buried, beside his wife, in the nave of Worcester Cathedral. Fifty-five years of unadventurous apprenticeship had led to fourteen years of leadership, buffeting but successful, crowned by a spectacular retirement, followed, ironically, for a man who set so much store by repose, by a sad decade of dismal leisure.

Biographical Appendix

L. S. AMERY (1873–1955), MP for the South (later Spark-brook) division of Birmingham (1910–45), occupied almost every 'imperial' Cabinet post in the last days of the British Empire. He was First Lord of the Admiralty (1922–4), Secretary of State for the Colonies (1924–9) and for the Dominions as well from 1925, Secretary of State for India (1940–5). He was a very short man, of high academic achievement, who had been an ardent tariff reformer, in season and out of season, from before even Joseph Chamberlain's conversion.

Max Aitken (1879–1964), cr. 1st Lord BEAVERBROOK 1917, was for most of his life an impish *voyeur* of politics, who used his newspaper more for mischief than for profit, let alone instruction. He was an arch-appeaser in the thirties but a dynamic Minister of Aircraft Production in 1940–1, before gradually returning to mischief for the latter part of the war and the subsequent peace. He was however a loyal friend (although mostly a bad advisor) to Churchill, who aroused his fealty more than anyone since Bonar Law – an odd pair to choose. This fealty certainly did not extend to Baldwin.

Frederick Edwin Smith (1872–1930), cr. knight 1915, baronet 1918, baron 1919, viscount 1921, 1st Earl of BIRKENHEAD 1922, was the archetypal thrusting lawyer politician who rumbustiously and ruthlessly sought 'the glittering prizes' (his own phrase in his somewhat notorious Glasgow Rectorial

Address of 1922). Conservative MP for the Walton division of Liverpool (1906–19), Solicitor-General (1915), Attorney-General (1915–19), Lord Chancellor (1919–22), Secretary of State for India (1924–8), he was gifted with a powerful physique which his excesses destroyed by the age of fifty-eight and a dialectical armoury which comprised bludgeons and rapiers in equal and unusual combination. Many thought that he had a cool head and good judgement as well. Churchill adored him (after Smith's death, thirty-five years before his own, he had no close associate who treated him as an equal) and paid a remarkable tribute to his courage and steadfastness in the foreword to a biography written by the 2nd Lord Birkenhead soon after the death of his father. The most recent and massively impressive study of Smith by John Campbell leaves a less favourable impression. It is not written destructively, but there can rarely have been a biography which more enhanced the reputation of the author and more damaged that of the subject.

Sir Arthur Griffith-BOSCAWEN, (1865–1946) was Minister of Agriculture for the last year of the Coalition Government. He lost his seat at Taunton, to which he had surprisingly switched from Dudley in 1921, at the 1922 election. He was nevertheless appointed Minister of Health by Bonar Law and, apparently after seventeen unsuccessful attempts to secure other nominations, was adopted as Conservative candidate for the by-election at Mitcham, where he was defeated by Labour as a result of the intervention of a Conservative Coalitionist. He never held office or achieved membership of the House of Commons again. With C. F. G. Masterman and Patrick Gordon Walker he was one of the very few British politicians of this century to lose his place in a Cabinet by personal electoral misfortune.

William Clive BRIDGEMAN (1864–1935), cr. 1st Viscount Bridgeman 1929, was the son of a country rector who was the younger son of an earl. MP for Oswestry (1906–29), Home

Secretary (1922–4), First Lord of the Admiralty (1924–9). He was a cricketer of quality who played in the Eton and Cambridge XIs and became President of the MCC.

George CAVE (1856–1928), cr. 1st Viscount Cave 1918, was MP for Kingston, Surrey (1906–18), a Chancery lawyer of note, Solicitor-General (1915–16), Home Secretary (1916–19), a Lord of Appeal (1919–22) and Lord Chancellor (1922–January 1924 and again from the end of 1924 until his death). His most notable electoral feat was his defeat of Asquith (by 987 votes to 441) for the Chancellorship of Oxford University when Curzon died in 1925. 'The greatest living Oxonian' (Birkenhead's campaigning description of Asquith – but Birkenhead had no reason to be pro-Cave, who had replaced him on the Woolsack when 'the cabin boys' took over from the admirals in 1922) was trounced by the least distinguished Lord Chancellor of the first thirty years of this century ('a brewers' lawyer', as he was derisively but inaccurately described by Asquith partisans). It showed the conservatism of the Oxford MAs in the twenties (on a very low poll), but also, probably, an unwillingness to allow a *parvenu* Liberal, even if of exceptional repute and gravitas, to be both Earl and Chancellor of Oxford.

Lord Robert CECIL (1864–1958), cr. Viscount Cecil of Chelwood 1923, was the third son of the 3rd Marquess of Salisbury (the Prime Minister), MP for Marylebone East (1906–10) and for Hitchin (1911–18), Lord Privy Seal (1923–4) and Chancellor of the Duchy of Lancaster (1924–7). It was from this last office, in which he was in effect Minister for League of Nations Affairs under Austen Chamberlain, that he resigned, holding the policy of the Government towards naval disarmament to be obstructive. Party politics sat lightly on his drooping shoulders. In 1921 he had been in negotiation with Grey and Asquith for the formation of a centre grouping and in 1924 he had been restrained with difficulty by his eldest brother from joining the Labour Government. His dominating concern was support for collective security. He was President of the League of Nations Union (1923–45), was awarded the Nobel Peace Prize in 1937, and gave his London house to Philip Noel-Baker, the Labour MP who was equally devoted to the Geneva cause.

Sir (Joseph) Austen CHAMBERLAIN (1863–1937), KG 1925, was the nearest approach to a man-made statesman there has been in modern British politics. The man who made him was his father, Joseph Chamberlain (1837–1914), an original politician of great flair, some of it destructive. Austen (to differentiate him from his father he was one of the first politicians to be habitually addressed and referred to by his Christian name) copied the eyeglass, orchid, wing collar, frock coat and hair parting of his father. He espoused his causes and even fell undemandingly in love with his father's third wife (formerly Miss Mary Endicott, the daughter of President Cleveland's Secretary of War, later Mrs Carnegie, who died only in 1957). Unfortunately, he inherited only the trappings. He was conventional and cautious, where his father had been daring and insolent. Beatrice Webb, who admittedly had half wanted to marry Joseph Chamberlain, thought Austen 'dull and closed-minded . . . intellectually dense' (*Diary*, vol. IV, page 70).

Despite his provenance he had no real roots in Birmingham, even though he represented it or its suburbs in Parliament for forty-five years, and divided his time between South Kensington and a small house in Sussex with a rock garden and the unfortunate name of Twitt's Ghyll. He was however a man of exceptional loyalty, decency, and, towards the end, experience. He was a junior minister (1895–1902), Postmaster-General (1902–3), Chancellor of the Exchequer (1903–5), Secretary of State for India (1915–17), Chancellor of the Exchequer (1919–21), Lord Privy Seal (1921–2), Foreign Secretary (1924–9), and First Lord of the Admiralty (August–October 1931). He was twice on the route to the Prime Ministership but did not press his own claims. In the memorable words of F. E. Smith, 'He always played the game and he always lost it.' An even more vivid portrait of him is conjured up by a mid-1920s incident at Polesdon Lacey, Mrs Ronald Greville's indulgent house in the Surrey hills. Displeased by the performance of her inebriated butler at dinner, she scribbled, 'You are very drunk; leave the room immediately' on a piece of paper and handed it to the miscreant servant, who mistily surveyed the room, decided without difficulty where the message would make most impact, and placed it first on a silver salver and then before Sir Austen Chamberlain.

Arthur James COOK (1885–1931) was born at Wookey in Somerset, the son of a regular soldier, but emigrated early to the Rhondda where he worked underground for twenty-one years. In 1918 he became a full-time union official and in 1924, succeeding the oversupple Frank Hodges, he became General Secretary of the Miners' Federation of Great Britain, then the largest trade union in the world. Cook, not dissimilar in appearance (but only appearance) from Mr Neil Kinnock, incited vast audiences, preferred oratory to negotiation, presided over a reduction of nearly 40 per cent in the membership of the MFGB, and drove himself into an early death at the age of forty-six.

Alfred Duff COOPER (1890–1954), cr. 1st Viscount Norwich 1952, began and ended his career as a diplomat, in the latter phase Ambassador to the French Committee of National Liberation (1943–4) and then to France (1944–7). In the interval he married Lady Diana Manners, was MP for Oldham (1924–9) and for St George's (1931–45). He was an irascible, high-living *flâneur*, who was much-loved by his coteries, a talented historical writer and a politician of courage, although an indifferent minister. He was Secretary of State for War (1935–7) and First Lord of Admiralty, (1937–8). Nothing became his occupancy of these service ministeries so much as

his leaving; he resigned over Munich. He was no more successful as Minister of Information in 1940–1, or in Singapore
before the invasion.

George Nathaniel CURZON (1859–1925), son and heir of the
4th Lord Scarsdale (to which title he succeeded in 1916), was
created Baron Curzon in the peerage of Ireland 1896 (and sat in
the House of Lords as an Irish Representative peer from 1908),
Earl Curzon of Kedleston 1911, and Marquess Curzon of
Kedleston 1921. He was Conservative MP for Southport from
1886 to 1898, when at the age of thirty-nine he was made
Viceroy of India, in which great office he experienced both
success and chagrin before returning home in some disorder in
1905. He led the 'hedgers' against the 'ditchers' in the Conservative split over the degree of House of Lords resistance to
the Parliament Bill in 1911, preferring retreat to the danger
of massive dilution of the peerage. He was Lord Privy Seal
(1915–16), Lord President and a member of the small War
Cabinet (1916–19), Foreign Secretary (1919–24), and Lord
President again from November 1924 until his death. He
married two rich Americans, one in 1895 and the second in
1917, and used their wealth to sustain the great titles and the
second and third country estates (at Hackwood and
Montacute) which he added to the Scarsdale inheritance at
Kedleston, but which all fell away with his death. He was a
highly intelligent but occasionally ridiculous grandee, a richly
anecdotal figure, devoted to public service, whose strength of
character did not match his imposing manners and appearance.

Ronald McNeill (1861–1936) was a Kent MP from 1911 until
he was created Lord CUSHENDUN in 1927 and entered the
Cabinet as Chancellor of the Duchy of Lancaster. Previously he
had been Financial Secretary to the Treasury under Churchill,
which was interesting, for McNeill's most famous parliamentary activity had been to throw a copy of the Standing Orders at

Churchill during an Irish Home Rule scene in November 1912, cutting his face quite badly.

J. C. C. DAVIDSON (1889–1970), cr. 1st Viscount Davidson 1937. Unpaid private secretary at the Colonial Office to Lord Crewe (1910) and Lewis Harcourt (1910–15); and to Bonar Law (1915–20) in successive offices. Conservative MP for Hemel Hempstead (1921–3 and 1924–37). Chancellor of the Duchy of Lancaster for most of Baldwin's periods of office. Chairman of the Conservative Party (1927–30). Married, 1919, to Joan (Mimi) Dickinson (died 1985), who succeeded him as MP for Hemel Hempstead (1937–59; herself a life peer as Baroness Northchurch from 1963), whom he had met through Baldwin, and to whom Baldwin remained devoted, as to Davidson, throughout his life.

Geoffrey DAWSON (1874–1944), editor of *The Times* (1912–19 and 1923– 41), was born Geoffrey Robinson but changed his name by Royal Licence in 1917 (a fashionable year for name changes: King George V moved from Saxe-Coburg-Gotha to Windsor) in order to inherit a substantial landed property in Yorkshire. He occupied the gap of 1919–23 as Estates Bursar of All Souls College, Oxford. *The Times* under Dawson was almost a great department of state rather than a mere newspaper and its editor almost an honorary member of the Cabinet. He gave lifelong adherence to his chosen heroes, Milner, Baldwin, Neville Chamberlain and Halifax. In his first editorship he wrote the leader which precipitated the fall of Asquith. Towards the close of his second he wrote the one which presaged the Munich agreement and the fall of Czechoslovakia.

Edward Stanley, 17th Earl of DERBY (1865–1948), Secretary of State for War, (1916–18 and 1922–4), Ambassador to Paris (1918–20). As a tribute to his great estates, personal popularity and regional political influence, he was sometimes called 'the

King of Lancashire'. Lloyd George, who used him a lot, found him more like a cushion which always bore the imprint of the last man who sat upon him. (This remark, however, is sometimes given other attributions both as to subject and to speaker.)

Victor Cavendish, 9th Duke of DEVONSHIRE (1868–1938), succeeded his uncle, the Marquess of Hartington of Liberal Unionism, in 1908. A junior minister (1903–5 and 1915–16), Governor-General of Canada (1916–21), where his ADC, Harold Macmillan, became engaged to his daughter, Lady Dorothy Cavendish, Secretary of State for the Colonies (1922–4). He occupied high office, but had less brio than most Dukes of Devonshire of the past hundred years.

Bolton EYRES-MONSELL (1880–1969), cr. 1st Viscount Monsell 1935, was a fellow Worcestershire MP with Baldwin for twenty-five of the latter's twenty-nine years in the House of Commons, sitting for the South or Evesham division from 1910 to 1935. He was a former naval officer who after twelve years in the Conservative Whips' Office, eight of them as Chief Whip, became First Lord of the Admiralty (1931–6).

Lord Edmund FITZALAN-Howard (1855–1947), younger son of the 14th Duke of Norfolk, changed his surname to Talbot in 1876 to comply with a will and then changed it back again in 1921 when he was created 1st Viscount FitzAlan of Derwent. He was MP for Chichester from 1894 to 1921 and Conservative Chief Whip for six years from 1915.

Sir Auckland Campbell GEDDES (1879–1954), cr. 1st Lord Geddes 1942. A former Professor of Anatomy at Edinburgh, Dublin, and McGill University, Montreal. He was a Lloyd George minister (President of the Board of Trade for the last year) before he went to Worthington for four years in 1920. His elder brother, Sir Eric Geddes, a railway engineer, was also a minister from 1917 to 1921, before becoming chairman of the Dunlop Rubber Company and of Imperial Airways. It was he, not Sir Auckland, who in 1918 promised to 'squeeze the German lemon until the pips squeak' and in 1922 wielded the 'Geddes axe'. The Geddes brothers were Lloyd George discoveries rather in the way that the Young brothers were Mrs Thatcher's.

Edward (Paddy) GOULDING (1862–1936), cr. Lord Wargrave 1922, was a rich businessman, later chairman of Rolls-Royce, MP for Devizes (1896–1906) and for Worcester City (1906–22). He was the owner of a luxurious Thames-side residence at Shiplake, where he became a backbench dispenser of hospitality and manipulator of politics of sufficient note to be made successively a baronet, a privy councillor and a peer by the Coalition Government. (He was lucky to achieve his honours before Baldwin became leader of the Conservative Party.) His father had been an Irish landowner.

Douglas McGarel Hogg (1872–1950), cr. 1st Viscount HAILSHAM 1928. Attorney-General (1922–4 [January] and 1924 [November] – 1928). Lord Chancellor (1928–9 and 1935–8). Secretary of State for War and Leader of the House of the Lords (1931–5). The son of Quintin Hogg the founder of the Regent Street Polytechnic and the father of Quintin Hogg (2nd Viscount Hailsham 1950–63, Mr Hogg again 1963–70 and Baron Hailsham of St Marylebone 1970; Lord Chancellor 1970–4 and 1979–).

Edward Wood (1881–1959), cr. Lord Irwin 1925, succeeded as 3rd Viscount HALIFAX 1934, cr. 1st Earl of Halifax 1944, KG, OM, was a dedicated, dignified and mostly far-sighted intendant of the declining years of British power. As Viceroy (1925–31) he saw the inevitability of Indian self-government. At the Foreign Office (Lord Privy Seal and then Lord President, 1935–8, and Secretary of State, February 1938–December

1940), he supported Chamberlain's policy of appeasement more out of pessimism than optimism. Nonetheless he was within a hair's breadth of becoming Prime Minister in May 1940. A lot of people who ought to have known better, from Herbert Morrison to Hugh Dalton, preferred him to Churchill at that stage. Fortunately, Halifax did not share their view. His third great post was as Ambassador to Washington (1941–6), where he played a notable role in getting the new world to redress the balance of the old. Baldwin had a great respect and regard for Halifax (or Wood as he then was) and made the inspired choice of sending him to Delhi. For the rest, however, he kept making him President of the Board of Education (1922–4 and 1932–5), a post which, despite being a Fellow of All Souls and Chancellor of the University of Oxford (1933–59), singularly failed to stir Halifax's imagination. While holding it he frequently hunted two days a week during the parliamentary session.

Sir Maurice HANKEY (1877–1963), cr. 1st Lord Hankey 1939, was a major of Marines when he became assistant secretary of the Committee of Imperial Defence in 1908. In 1912 he became secretary of that body. In 1916 he became the first secretary of the (War) Cabinet. Both these posts he held until he retired in 1938, adding to them the clerkship of the Privy Council in 1923. So indispensable had he become that he was recalled to serve in Chamberlain's Cabinet in 1939 and continued as a minister under Churchill until 1942. With perfect impartiality he dedicated his memoir of *The Supreme Command* (in World War I) to Balfour, Asquith and Lloyd George.

Alexander HARDINGE (1894–1960). In 1944 he succeeded his father who had been twice permanent under-secretary of the Foreign Office on either side of being Viceroy of India (1910–1916) as 2nd Lord Hardinge of Penshurst. He was a full-time courtier from 1920 to 1943, and a part-time one for the rest of his life. He served King George V, King Edward VIII, King

George VI and the present Queen. He had not been with the King as Prince of Wales, but had sixteen years' training as assistant private secretary to King George V. They had not been lost upon him.

Sir Samuel HOARE (1880–1959), cr. 1st and only Viscount Templewood 1944. He was MP for Chelsea (1910–44), Secretary of State for Air (1922–4 and 1924–9), Secretary of State for India (1931–5), Foreign Secretary (disastrously) in 1935, First Lord of the Admiralty (1936–7), Home Secretary (1937–9), Lord Privy Seal (1939–40), Secretary of State for Air (again) (1940) and Ambassador to Spain (1940–4). He was never a close friend of Baldwin's – I think he was too dapper and quick on his feet (President of the National Skating Federation) for the leader's ideal taste, but he was a central man of government of the Baldwin era, adaptable and available. He was notably liberal on Indian and on penal questions at the Home Office, but acquired a perhaps unfair reactionary reputation as a result of the 'Hoare-Laval Pact' (pages 139–43 *supra*) and his wartime mission to General Franco.

Sir Robert HORNE (1871–1940) cr. 1st and only Viscount Horne 1937. MP for the Hillhead division of Glasgow, 1918–37. Chancellor of the Exchequer, 1921–2. A son of the manse and educated entirely in Scotland, his only address for the last decades of his life was 69 Arlington House, Piccadilly, London, W1. A bachelor, he was addicted to nightclubs. Baldwin did not like him, and referred to him as 'that rare thing – a Scots cad' (Middlemas and Barnes, *Baldwin*, page 282).

Sir Thomas INSKIP (1876–1947), cr. 1st Viscount Caldecote 1939, was a notable lawyer, a KC since 1914, and a churchman of firm evangelical persuasion. He was a Law Officer for most of the fourteen years from 1922 to 1936, unusually reverting to being Solicitor after having been Attorney when the National Government was formed in 1931, but becoming Attorney

again in 1932. After three years as Minister for the Coordination of Defence (1936–9), which was a non-job with no
department and few staff, he was elevated on the outbreak of
war to become Lord Chancellor (although to be moved from
Defence when a war begins is not perhaps the greatest compli-
ment). In May 1940 he had to be moved again in order to make
room for Simon on the Woolsack as Churchill wished to
exclude his colleague in pre-1914 Liberal Cabinets from any
part in the direction of the war without humiliating him.
Happily for Inskip a vacancy was possible on the traditional
'Attorney-General's pillow' of the Lord Chief Justiceship of
England, which he occupied for the next six years. He was
however the end of the tradition. No subsequent Attorney has
become Lord Chief Justice. Nor had anyone before him gone to
the Chief Justiceship via the Woolsack.

Dr Thomas JONES, CH (1870–1955) was both an important
chronicler of Baldwin's reaction to events and a valued and
sympathetic confidant. He was the eldest son of the storekeep-
er of the mining 'company shop' at Rhymney, the only Welsh-
speaking part of Monmouthshire. He left school at thirteen but
then got himself to the University College of Wales at Abery-
stwyth, before proceeding to Glasgow University, where he
stayed as student and lecturer for fifteen years. Then he became
briefly Professor of Economics at Queen's University, Belfast.
He went back to Wales as a protégé of David Davies of Llandi-
nam, almost the only philanthropic Welsh coal-owner, and his
sisters, the Misses Davies of Gregynog, who combined spinster-
hood with the accumulation of a remarkable collection of
French impressionists, which today repose (when not in
Japan) in the National Museum of Wales in Cardiff. Through
the Davies family he met Lloyd George, who inducted him to
Whitehall in 1916, first as assistant then as deputy secretary of
the Cabinet. The creation of a Liberal Prime Minister, Jones cast
a gentle Labour vote throughout his life, but got along best with
his Conservative masters, first with Bonar Law and then, much

more strongly, with Baldwin. On his retirement in 1930 he became secretary and later chairman of the Pilgrim Trust. He founded Coleg Harlech, the adult education college in Merionethshire. Some people would say that, after Lloyd George, he was the greatest Welshman of the first half of this century, others that he was a little Welsh toady. I think that his relationship with Baldwin is perfectly expressed by the photograph reproduced between pages 64 and 65.

Sir William JOYNSON-HICKS (1865–1937), cr. 1st Viscount Brentford 1929. A prosperous solicitor, widely known as Jix, he was very keen on motoring and on police raids to seize the works of such notorious pornographic authors as Radcliffe Hall and D. H. Lawrence.

Cosmo Gordon LANG (1864–1945), Archbishop of Canterbury (1928–42), cr. Lord Lang of Lambeth 1942, had a perfectly shaped ecclesiastical career. Ordained in 1891, he was vicar of the University Church at Oxford (1894–6), then for five years of Portsea (in Portsmouth), which for 100 years bred bishops as Whitstable bred oysters, then suffragan Bishop of Stepney (1901–9). Then (a great step at the age of forty-five) Archbishop of York, then of Canterbury nineteen years later. He also had an almost perfectly shaped ecclesiastical face, the best since Cardinal Manning. Unlike Manning, however, he did not start in the Church of England. His father was a Scots Presbyterian, Principal of Aberdeen University and sometime Minister of Anderston, Glasgow. Neither these attributes nor his presidency of the Oxford Union and fellowship of All Souls prevented his being widely regarded as an unctuous prelate. After a censorious broadcast at the time of the Abdication (a year later), Gerald Bullett (1893–1958, prolific author and general man of letters) wrote a satirical quatrain which was almost the last example of the bitter political verse which, with differing prejudices and rhythms, Kipling, Belloc and Chesterton had produced a generation before:

>My Lord Archbishop what a scold you are!
>And when your man is down how bold you are!
>Of Christian charity how scant you are!
>And auld Lang swine how full of Cantuar!

Sir David LOW (1891–1963), knighted 1962, was a New Zealander who came to London in 1919 and did his most notable work, including the creation of Colonel Blimp, on Beaverbrook's *Evening Standard* from 1922 to 1950. He shared little of his proprietor's outlook except for his irreverence. He was the most notable political cartoonist of his generation.

Captain David MARGESSON (1890–1965), cr. 1st Viscount Margesson 1942, was MP for West Ham (1922–3) and for Rugby (1924–42). He served in the Conservative Whips' office for sixteen of his eighteen years as member for Rugby and was Chief Whip 1931–40. Churchill in 1940 surprisingly rewarded this organizer of the solid Baldwin and Chamberlain majorities of the 'years of unpreparedness' by making him Secretary of State for War (1940–2).

Major-General Sir Frederick MAURICE (1871–1951) was a Cambridge intellectual (the grandson of F. D. Maurice, one of the founders of Christian Socialism, and the father of Joan Robinson, the economist) who as a professional and successful soldier played a significant if inadvertent part in the break-up of the Liberal Party. As Director of Military Operations at the War Office in 1918 he publicly accused the Prime Minister of inaccurate statements about the strength of the army in France. In the House of Commons debate which followed, Asquith voted for the first time against the Lloyd George Government. Those Liberals who voted with him were refused 'the coupon' at the general election at the end of that year.

Reginald McKENNA (1863–1943). MP for North Monmouthshire (1895–1918). Financial Secretary to the Treasury (1905–

7), President of the Board of Education (1907–8), First Lord of the Admiralty (1908–11), Home Secretary (1911–15), Chancellor of the Exchequer (1915–16), chairman of Midland Bank (1919–43). I find him one of the most insubstantial figures of the first half of the twentieth century. He sat in Parliament for twenty-three years for the constituency (in 1918 renamed Pontypool, now foolishly re-renamed Torfaen) in which I was brought up and which my father subsequently represented; he held two great offices of state (Home Secretary and Chancellor) which I was subsequently to occupy; he was one of the three or four closest governmental friends of Asquith, about whom I have written at length; yet for me he has no more solidity than the powdered wings of a butterfly. McKenna, however, was never crushed. He was always successful, sought after, but without substance. The 1948 biography of him by his nephew Stephen McKenna, successful and prolific novelist, lacks shape, style, photographs and an index. It is no good on his provenance (surely a nepotic biography should have managed that), his beliefs, his wife or why as an ex-senior minister and chairman of a major bank for twenty-four years he never became a peer. Perhaps he always wished to be available to be offered the Chancellorship, even if not to accept.

Sir Walter MONCKTON, KC (1891–1965), cr. 1st Viscount Monckton of Brenchley 1957. He was a highly agreeable and talented lawyer who believed in accommodation rather than confrontation, and was appropriately Minister of Labour in the second Churchill Government. Less appropriately he was Minister of Defence in the subsequent Eden Government. He disapproved of the Suez adventure, but, true to his desire for accommodation, allowed himself to be moved sideways (and a little downward) to the Chancellorship of the Duchy of Lancaster, rather than resigning. He left politics three months later, and like a number of other politicians found the Midland Bank eager to welcome him as chairman. In the thirties, he waxed rich by advising the Nizam of Hyderabad and famous by advising King Edward VIII, to whom, as Prince of Wales, he had become Attorney-General in 1932.

J. T. C. MOORE-BRABAZON (1884–1964), cr. 1st Lord Brabazon 1942, was a racing driver and pioneer aviator who held the first British pilot's licence and was five times decorated in 1914–18. He was a Cresta Run tobogganist and a golfer of note. He was MP for Chatham (1918–29) and, in spite of his dodging of St George's, for Wallasey (1931–42). He was Minister of Transport (1940–1) and Minister of Aircraft Production (1941–2). In 1946 he had an enormous but ineffective aeroplane, a sort of whale of the air, named after him. He was altogether a man of parts. His unwillingness to stand at St George's could not easily be put down to cowardice.

Sir Oswald MOSLEY (1896–1981), succeeded as 6th baronet in 1928. He was married to a daughter of Lord Curzon from 1920 to 1933 when she died, and then to Diana Mitford. He was MP for Harrow, first as a Conservative and then as an independent (1918–23), and Labour MP for Smethwick (1926–31). He was Chancellor of the Duchy of Lancaster (outside the Cabinet) in 1929–30. He then resigned and founded the New Party, which had respectable adherents until in 1932 it became the British Union of Fascists. He was a charismatic vulgarian, a visionary who organized thugs, an improbable Wykehamist, who was imprisoned for three and a half years during the Second World War as a danger to the state.

Sir Harold NICOLSON (1886–1968) was the younger son of the 1st Lord Carnock (Ambassador to St Petersburg and permanent under-secretary at the Foreign Office) and the husband of Vita Sackville-West. He was himself a diplomat until the age of forty-three, but then resigned and devoted himself to literature, broadcasting, social life and politics. For all of these, except the last, he had a high talent. Unfortunately it was the exception which most excited his interest. After a brief spell in Oswald Mosley's New Party he joined MacDonald's National Labour Party, was MP for Leicester West (1935–45) and rose to be an ill-regarded parliamentary secretary to the Ministry of Information (1940–1). After his defeat in 1945 he tried hard to get back to Parliament. He could not bear to see the light shining above Big Ben and indicating that the House from which he was excluded was still sitting. He was however fairly open-minded about which Chamber he joined. He fought an unsuccessful by-election for the Labour Party in 1948, and then greatly hoped for a peerage which never came. He was knighted for writing an authorized but elegant life of King George V. His three volumes of *Diaries and Letters*, although they were not his best work, made him a noted chronicler of the thirties, forties and fifties.

Montagu NORMAN (1871–1950), cr. Lord Norman of St Clere 1944, was Governor of the Bank of England from 1920 to 1944, an unprecedented span. He was educated at Eton and King's College, Cambridge, as, twelve years behind him, was his frequent adversary, Maynard Keynes. Norman was in no way a Blimp, his intellect was almost as supple (although not as innovative) as Keynes's. He was unfortunately mostly wrong. Mr Peregrine Worsthorne, editor of the *Sunday Telegraph*, is his stepson.

Ronald Munro-Ferguson (1860–1934), cr. 1st and only Viscount NOVAR 1920, had been a Liberal MP for thirty years until he went to Australia as Governor-General in 1914. Sometime after his return in 1920 he slipped over to the Conservatives. He was Secretary for Scotland (the Secretaryship of State was not created until 1927) in the first Baldwin Government.

Sir Arthur PUGH (1870–1955), General Secretary of the British Iron and Steel and Kindred Trades Association (1917–36), was in 1935 (together with Sir Walter [later Lord] Citrine), one of the first trade union leaders to be knighted. He began a current of fashion which flowed with mounting strength for forty years and then dried up. He was the epitome in substance and manner of a moderate union leader, and as great a contrast with Cook or Smith as it is possible to imagine.

Sir John REITH (1889–1971), cr. 1st Lord Reith 1940, was Manager and later Director-General of the BBC from 1922 to 1938. Then he became chairman of Imperial Airways and its successor BOAC. Between 1940 and 1942 he was an MP (for Southampton) for a few months, then a peer, and successively Minister of Information, Minister of Transport, Minister of Works and Buildings and Minister of Works and Planning. Churchill was unimpressed by his towering appearance and self-righteous confidence. 'Keep that wuthering height away from me,' he said. But it took him two years to get Reith, who then became a Lieutenant-Commander RNVR, out of his Government. Reith's diaries, published posthumously, showed distinct signs of paranoia. He was so eager to become Ambassador to Washington in 1940 that he records how he spent a journey home to the Chilterns trying, in an almost telephonic sense, to arrange for divine intervention: 'Keep trying to be in touch with God about the USA business' (*The Reith Diaries*, p. 270).

Harold Sidney Harmsworth (1868–1940), cr. 1st Lord ROTH-ERMERE 1914, and 1st Viscount 1919, after a year as Lloyd George's Air Minister. The brother of Lord Northcliffe, the uncle of Cecil King, thus at the core of the new press purple of the first two-thirds of this century. His principal organ was the *Daily Mail*, although he had many subsidiary ones. In the twenties, he became involved with the cause of the (right-wing) regime in Hungary, to such an extent that the Admiral Horthy offered him the throne. In the thirties he and the *Daily Mail* flirted with Mussolini and Mosley.

James Cecil, 4th Marquess of SALISBURY (1861–1947). MP for Darwen and then Rochester (1885–1903). Holder of various Cabinet offices, mostly without portfolio, between 1905 and 1929. Leader of the House of Lords (1925–9). He was the son of the Prime Minister, and the eldest brother of Lord Hugh Cecil (Lord Quickswood), Lord Robert Cecil (Viscount Cecil of Chelwood, *q.v.*), and Lord William Cecil, Bishop of Exeter, 1916–36.

Herbert SAMUEL (1870–1963), GCB 1926, cr. 1st Viscount 1937, OM 1958, was MP for Cleveland (1902–18) and for Darwen (1929–35). He held various minor Cabinet offices before being briefly Home Secretary in 1916, and again in 1931–2. He was leader of the Liberal Party from 1931 to 1935. He was British High Commissioner in Palestine (1920–5) which together with his Liverpool birth accounted for the fact that he somewhat incongruously became Lord Samuel of Mount Carmel and Toxteth. He was stronger on gravitas and intellect than on flair. With, most notably, Haldane, Halifax and Waverley, he has been one of eight non-Prime Ministerial politicians to receive the Order of Merit (the order was created in 1902 and of Prime Ministers since that date five out of seventeen have had it bestowed upon them).

John SANKEY (1866–1948), High Court Judge from 1914, cr. Lord Sankey 1929, and Viscount 1932, Lord Chancellor, 1929–35, appears to have been a remarkably dull man. A High Anglican bachelor from Lancing College (and Jesus College, Oxford), he showed no sign of the feline wit which such a provenance might have been expected to produce. He made no recorded memorable remark or memorable judgment, except for his extracurricular report on the Coal Industry in 1919. He was a broad-cloth lawyer who achieved limited authority through silence. By comparison his successors as Labour Lord Chancellors, still more his only predecessor, appear scintillating.

Herbert SMITH (1861–1938) was President of the Miners' Federation (1922–9). In an age when many miners' leaders (but not A. J. Cook) looked and dressed more like senior divines or Southern American senators than like Mr Arthur Scargill, he stuck firmly to a flat-cap unflamboyant image. He was the no-nonsense man who growled while Cook spouted, whose word was trusted and not only because he spoke so few. He resigned abruptly from the presidency in 1929 and was succeeded by the Right Honourable Thomas Richards, a former MP and Lloyd George Privy Councillor, who was much more in the patriarchal tradition.

Sir Donald SOMERVELL (1889–1960), cr. Lord Somervell of Harrow (Life Peer) 1954, when he became a Lord of Appeal in Ordinary, Solicitor-General (1933–6), Attorney-General (1936–45), Home Secretary, briefly and almost secretly in the 'Caretaker' Government of the summer of 1945. He held all his offices unobtrusively, although not all briefly. He was Attorney-General for a longer period than any man for 150 years past. He was the son of a Harrow master whom Churchill claimed taught him to write good English (Colville, *Fringes of Power*, page 483n.). This did not however cause Churchill to write much of it about the son, whose Attorney-Generalship brought him only eight cursory references in the six volumes of *The Second World War*.

Arthur John Bigge (1849–1931), cr. 1st and only Lord STAM-FORDHAM 1911, was born the fourth son of a country vicar and became a quintessential courtier. He was still serving King George V fifty-one years after he had been appointed assistant private secretary to Queen Victoria. He was a clever, devoted, peppery man of whom Mr Kenneth Rose wrote that '[his] letters were cast in a formal language which lent itself more to rebuke than to encouragement' (*King George V*, page 371).

Sir Arthur STEEL-MAITLAND, Bart (1876–1935) had indeed

had a remarkable Oxford career. He got a First in Mods, a First in Greats, followed by a First in Law. He was President of the Union, a rowing blue, and a Fellow of All Souls. His political career was less remarkable. He became the fourth Member from a Birmingham constituency in the Cabinet, for what was then the Erdington division.

James Henry (Jimmy) THOMAS (1874–1949) was as typically Georgian a figure as Elgar was an Edwardian and Tennyson a Victorian. But he was closer to his sovereign than was either the composer or the poet. King George V was long thought to have cleared up a 1929 chest abcess by excessive laughter at one of Thomas's jokes. Thomas, like Baldwin, was a man of the Great Western Railway. He was born in Newport and lived his early adult life in Swindon. In 1910 he celebrated King George's accession by becoming both Secretary of the Amalgamated Society of Railway Servants (later the National Union of Railwaymen) and Member of Parliament for Derby (an ecumenical gesture towards the Midland Railway). A year after the end of the King's reign (in 1937) Thomas suffered the humiliation of being forced to resign both as minister and MP as a result of the betrayal of a budget secret for commercial gain. In the interval he held three Cabinet offices, followed MacDonald without hesitation into the National Government of 1931, and, somewhat incongruously and almost uniquely amongst British politicians, was given honorary degrees by both Oxford and Cambridge. He was the author of one of the most impudently successful replies to a heckler ever recorded. 'You've sold us,' an affronted delegate called out at an NUR Conference. 'I tried to, but I couldn't get a bid,' he replied.

Sir Robert TOPPING (1877–1952), a Dublin Unionist who after twenty-four years as a peripatetic Conservative agent became the chief official of the party in 1928 and remained in the job until 1945. Knighted in 1934.

Sir William George TYRRELL (1866–1947), cr. 1st and only Lord Tyrrell of Avon 1929. He was private secretary to Sir Edward Grey (1907–15), permanent under-secretary (1925–8), and Ambassador to Paris (1928–34). His name (and his signature) attained wide public recognition when in the plenitude of the cinema age he was President of the British Board of Film Censors from 1935 to 1947. His relative lack of distinction did not prevent his being very adequately decorated. He was made CB in 1909, KCMG in 1913, KCVO in 1919, GCMG in 1925, KCB in 1927, a Privy Councillor in 1928, a peer in 1929 and GCB in 1934.

Sir Robert VANSITTART (1881–1957), cr. Lord Vansittart 1941, was Foreign Office permanent under-secretary (1930–8), then shunted to be chief diplomatic advisor (1938–41). This was because of his determined anti-German views, which got in the way of Chamberlain's policy of the appeasement of Hitler. These views, however, were based much more on anti-Teutonic prejudice than on ideology. He was rather favourable to Mussolini's Italy. He wrote twenty-four books, giving most of them unfortunate titles.

Lieutenant-Colonel Sir Ronald WATERHOUSE (1878–1942) was a regular soldier who found his way into 10 Downing Street with Bonar Law, who however considerably disliked him. He then remained as principal private secretary for six years, serving three Prime Ministers, despite some evidence that he was not much good at the job (see H. Montgomery Hyde's *Baldwin*, page 148). When he left government service at the age of fifty, he became a pilot officer in the RAF Volunteer Reserve and married as his second wife Nourah Chard who had been Mrs Baldwin's secretary and published around the date of his death an account of these 1923 events which was strongly objected to and in effect censored by Buckingham Palace. There remains an impression of something slightly odd about Waterhouse.

Tom WILLIAMS (1888–1967), MP for Don Valley (1922–59), cr. Lord Williams of Barnburgh, 1961. A miner whose contribution to the post-1940 revival of British agriculture made him almost a rival in husbandry to Coke of Norfolk or 'Turnip' Townshend. He was parliamentary secretary to the Ministry of Agriculture throughout the Churchill coalition, and Minister of Agriculture throughout the Attlee Government. His dress indicated neither his origin nor his devotion to the land; he never appeared in public except in wing collar, bow tie and pin-striped suit.

Sir Horace WILSON (1882–1972) entered the Civil Service at the age of eighteen, but rose to be permanent secretary to the Ministry of Labour (1921–30), chief industrial advisor to the Government (1930–9), and was seconded to the Treasury from 1935 to advise Neville Chamberlain, and when the latter became Prime Minister in 1937, became increasingly his chief foreign policy advisor. He was consequently heavily tarred with the appeasement brush. In Hugh Dalton's *War Diaries*, for instance, by the time of which he had become joint permanent secretary to the Treasury (1939–42), he was constantly referred to as 'Sir H. Quisling'.

George Malcolm YOUNG (1882–1959), Oxford historian and Fellow of All Souls. His published works covered an unusually wide range of centuries. With the subject's encouragement he wrote the first posthumous life of Baldwin. It was not a book which anyone would have wished to have commissioned about himself. It was remarkably short for a semi-official life of a man who was three times Prime Minister. It was also arguably 'poor, nasty, and brutish', although 'solitary', Hobbes's fifth adjective about the life of man, was inapplicable. On the only occasion that I met Young, immediately following the publication of his biography in 1952, I conversationally opined that Baldwin must have been a man of great charm. 'No,' Young

said, 'I never found him so. I much preferred Neville Chamberlain.'

Sir George YOUNGER (1851–1929), cr. 1st Viscount Younger
of Leckie, 1923. MP for Ayr Burghs (1906–22), Chairman of
the Conservative Party (1916–23). It was he who primarily
occasioned Birkenhead's jibe about 'cabin boys' (see page 52
supra). As a former Liverpool Unionist lawyer MP, Birkenhead
ought to have had more respect for such a notable brewer.

Notes

Introduction

1. Hansard, vol. 270, col. 632, 10 Nov. 1932.
2. Hansard, vol. 317, col. 1144, Nov. 1936.

1. A Quiet Beginning

1. *The Times*, 22 May 1950.
2. Davidson Papers, quoted in Middlemas and Barnes, *Baldwin*, p. 660.
3. Thomas Jones, *Whitehall Diary*, vol. 1, p. 255.
4. Quoted in Middlemas and Barnes, *op. cit.*, p. 41.

2. The Leap to Fame

1. Quoted in Middlemas and Barnes, *op. cit.*, p. 71.
2. ibid, p. 68.
3. A. W. Baldwin, *My Father: the True Story*, p. 114.
4. Baldwin Papers 42 ff. 3–10.
5. Thomas Jones, *op. cit.*, vol. 1, p. 227.
6. Hansard, vol. 160, col. 561, 16 Feb. 1923.
7. Robert Rhodes James, ed., *Memoirs of a Conservative*, p. 154.
8. Middlemas and Barnes, *op. cit.*, p. 162.
9. ibid, p. 169.

3. An Unsettled Leadership

1. Thomas Jones, *op. cit.*, vol. 1, p. 256.
2. A. W. Baldwin, *op. cit.*, p. 122.
3. G. M. Young, *Stanley Baldwin*, p. 72.
4. ibid, p. 57.
5. Chamberlain Papers, 1/27/72.
6. Jones Papers, 25 Nov. 1943.
7. There was no authentic text. This is from the notes for the speech quoted in Middlemas and Barnes, *op. cit.*, p. 229, and written at 3 Elliot Terrace (the Astor house), Plymouth Hoe.
8. *The Leo Amery Diaries*, p. 351.
9. Quoted in Middlemas and Barnes, *op. cit.*, pp. 240–1.
10. Thomas Jones, *op. cit.*, vol. 1, p. 257.
11. Quoted in Robert Rhodes James, *op. cit.*, p. 192.
12. Thomas Jones, *op. cit.*, vol. 1, p. 265.
13. Quoted in G. M. Young, *op. cit.*, p. 71.
14. Letter to Hilda Chamberlain, 9 Feb. 1924.
15. Thomas Jones, *op. cit.*, vol. 1, pp. 275–6.
16. ibid, p. 301.
17. ibid, p. 303.
18. idem.

4. The Perplexity of Power

1. Letter of 10 Oct. 1928 quoted in Birkenhead, *F.E.*, p. 545.
2. Quoted in Middlemas and Barnes, *op. cit.*, p. 343.
3. Hansard, vol. 181, col. 840
4. G. M. Young, *op. cit.*, p. 99.
5. ibid, p. 103.
6. Thomas Jones, *op. cit.*, vol. 1, p. 330.
7. ibid, vol. 2, p. 19.
8. ibid, pp. 21–3.
9. ibid, p. 23.

10. ibid, pp. 28–9.
11. Thomas Jones, *op. cit.*, vol. 2, p. 38.
12. Keith Feiling, *The Life of Neville Chamberlain*, p. 162.
13. Thomas Jones, *op. cit.*, vol. 2, p. 86.
14. ibid, vol. 2, p. 88.

5. The Defeat of 'Safety First'

1. Thomas Jones, *op. cit.*, vol. 2, p. 143
2. ibid, p. 186.
3. Letter to Sir William Wyndham, 1716.
4. Papers of Sir John Elliot (son of *Daily Express* editor, R. D. Blumfeld), quoted in Middlemas and Barnes, *op. cit.*, p. 579.
5. Hansard, vol. 231, col. 1306, 7 Nov. 1929.
6. Robert Rhodes James, *op. cit.*, p. 357 *et seq.*
7. Hansard, vol. 249, col. 1426, 12 March 1930.
8. Quoted in Young, *op. cit.*, p. 92.

6. The National Government

1. Keith Feiling, *op. cit.*, p. 189.
2. Iain Macleod, *Neville Chamberlain*, p. 149.
3. Quoted in Middlemas and Barnes, *op. cit.*, p. 621.
4. Robert Rhodes James, *op cit.*, p. 367.
5. ibid, p. 368.
6. Templewood, *Nine Troubled Years*, p. 18.
7. Harold Nicolson, *King George V*, p. 462.
8. Robert Rhodes James, *op. cit.*, p. 370.
9. Quoted in Middlemas and Barnes, *op. cit.*, p. 640.
10. Herbert Samuel, *Memoirs*, p. 214.
11. Templewood, *op. cit.*, p. 178.

12. Thomas Jones, *A Diary with Letters*, p. 155.
13. Quoted in Middlemas and Barnes, op. cit., p. 640.
14. Hansard, vol. 307, col. 856, 10 Dec. 1935.
15. Templewood, *op. cit.*, p. 185.
16. H. Montgomery Hyde, *op. cit.*, p. 412.
17. Idem.
18. Quoted in Middlemas and Barnes, *op. cit.*, p. 894.
19. Quoted in H. Montgomery Hyde, *op. cit.*, p. 412.
20. Robert Rhodes James, *op. cit.*, p. 411.
21. ibid.

7. Abdication and Retirement

1. Thomas Jones, *A Diary with Letters*, p. 162.
2. Quoted in Middlemas and Barnes, *op. cit.*, p. 978.
3. Anthony Eden, *Facing the Dictators*, p. 410.
4. Quoted in Frances Donaldson, *Edward VIII*, p. 238.
5. G. M. Young, *op. cit.*, p. 243.
6. Idem.
7. Quoted in Middlemas and Barnes, *op. cit.*, p. 1013.
8. Harold Nicolson, *Diaries and Letters, 1930–9*, p. 286.
9. Thomas Jones, *A Diary with Letters*, p. 297.
10. Quoted in H. Montgomery Hyde, *op. cit.*, p. 568.
11. ibid, p. 446.
12. Hansard, vol. 317, col. 1144, 12 Nov. 1936.
13. Letter from Baldwin to J. P. L. Thomas, quoted in Montgomery Hyde, *op. cit.*, p. 537.
14. Thomas Jones, *A Diary with Letters*, p. 325.

Select Bibliography

Baldwin books
(in chronological order of publication)

Stanley Baldwin, *On England*, Philip Allan, 1926
A. G. Whyte, *Stanley Baldwin. A Biographical Character Study*,
    Chapman and Hall, 1926
Wickham Steed, *The Real Stanley Baldwin*, Nisbet, 1930
Arthur Bryant, *Stanley Baldwin*, Hamish Hamilton, 1937
G. M. Young, *Stanley Baldwin*, Rupert Hart-Davis, 1952
D. C. Somervell, *Stanley Baldwin. An Examination of Some Features of
    G. M. Young's Biography*, Faber and Faber, 1953
A. W. Baldwin, *My Father: the True Story*, Allen and Unwin, 1955
John Raymond (ed.), *The Baldwin Age*, Eyre and Spottiswoode, 1960
Keith Middlemas and John Barnes, *Baldwin*, Weidenfeld and
    Nicolson, 1969
H. Montgomery Hyde, *Baldwin: the Unexpected Prime Minister*,
    Hart-Davis, MacGibbon, 1973
Kenneth Young, *Baldwin*, Weidenfeld and Nicolson, 1976

Autobiographies and biographies of other people
(in alphabetical order of subject)

J. Barnes and D. Nicholson (eds.), *The Leo Amery Diaries*, vol. 1,
    1896–1929, Hutchinson, 1980
J. A. Spender and Cyril Asquith, *The Life of Herbert Henry Asquith,
    Lord Oxford and Asquith*, 2 vols., Hutchinson, 1932
Roy Jenkins, *Asquith*, Collins, 1964 (3rd edition, 1986)
Stephen Koss, *Asquith*, Allen Lane, 1976
Roy Jenkins, *Mr Attlee. An Interim Biography*, Heinemann, 1948
Kenneth Harris, *Attlee*, Weidenfeld and Nicolson, 1982
Trevor Burridge, *Clement Attlee. A Political Biography*, Jonathan Cape,
    1985

Blanche E. C. Dugdale, *Arthur James Balfour, 1st Earl of Balfour*, 2 vols., Hutchinson, 1936

Kenneth Young, *Arthur James Balfour*, Bell, 1963

Max Egremont, *Balfour*, Collins, 1980

A. J. P. Taylor, *Beaverbrook*, Hamish Hamilton, 1972

Alan Bullock, *The Life and Times of Ernest Bevin*, vol. 1, *Trade Union Leader*, Heinemann, 1960

2nd Earl of Birkenhead, *F.E. The Life of F. E. Smith, 1st Earl of Birkenhead* (revised edition), Eyre and Spottiswoode, 1960

John Campbell, *F. E. Smith, 1st Earl of Birkenhead*, Jonathan Cape, 1984

R. A. Butler, *The Art of the Possible. The Memoirs of Lord Butler*, Hamish Hamilton, 1971

Charles Petrie, *The Life and Letters of the Right Honourable Sir Austen Chamberlain*, 2 vols., Cassell, 1939 and 1940

David Dutton, *Austen Chamberlain: Gentleman in Politics*, Ross Anderson, 1985

D. R. Thorpe, *The Uncrowned Prime Ministers: Austen Chamberlain, Curzon and R. A. Butler*, Darkhorse Publishing, 1980

Keith Feiling, *Life of Neville Chamberlain*, Macmillan, 1946

Iain Macleod, *Neville Chamberlain*, Frederick Muller, 1961

David Dilks, *Neville Chamberlain*, vol. 1, *1869–1929*, Cambridge University Press, 1984

Robert Rhodes James (ed.), *Chips. The Diaries of Sir Henry Channon*, Weidenfeld and Nicolson, 1967

Robert Rhodes James, *Churchill: a Study in Failure, 1900–1939*, Weidenfeld and Nicolson, 1970

Martin Gilbert, *Winston S. Churchill*, vol. V, *1922–1939*, Heinemann, 1976

Duff Cooper, *Old Men Forget*, Hart-Davis, 1953

John Charmley, *Duff Cooper: the Authorized Biography*, Weidenfeld and Nicolson, 1986

Harold Nicolson, *Curzon: the Last Phase*, Constable, 19

Leonard Mosley, *Curzon: the End of an Epoch*, Longman, 1960

Kenneth Rose, *Superior Person* (Curzon, 1859–98), Weidenfeld and Nicolson, 1969

Robert Rhodes James (ed.), *Memoirs of a Conservative: J. C. C. Davidson's Memoirs and Papers, 1910–37*, Weidenfeld and Nicolson, 1969

Randolph S. Churchill, *Lord Derby: King of Lancashire*, Heinemann, 1959

Anthony Eden, *Facing the Dictators*, Cassell, 1962

David Carlton, *Anthony Eden: a Biography*, Allen Lane, 1981

Robert Rhodes James, *Anthony Eden*, Weidenfeld and Nicolson, 1986

Frances Donaldson, *Edward VIII*, Weidenfeld and Nicolson, 1974
HRH the Duke of Windsor, *A King's Story*, Cassell, 1951
Duchess of Windsor, *The Heart Has Its Reasons*, Michael Joseph, 1956
Harold Nicolson, *King George V: His Life and Reign*, Constable, 1952
Kenneth Rose, *King George V*, Weidenfeld and Nicolson, 1983
John Wheeler-Bennett, *King George VI: His Life and Reign*,
    Macmillan, 1958
Keith Robbins, *Sir Edward Grey: a Biography of Lord Grey of Falloden*,
    Cassell, 1971
Earl of Halifax, *Fullness of Days*, Collins, 1957
2nd Earl of Birkenhead, *Halifax*, Hamish Hamilton, 1965
Samuel Hoare (Lord Templewood), *The Unbroken Thread*, Collins,
    1949
Samuel Hoare (Lord Templewood), *Nine Troubled Years*, Collins,
    1954
Thomas Jones, *A Diary with Letters, 1931–50*, Oxford University
    Press, 1954
Thomas Jones, *Whitehall Diary*, vol. I, *1916–25*; vol. II, *1926–30*,
    Oxford University Press, 1969 and 1971
Robert Blake, *The Unknown Prime Minister: the Life and Times of
    Andrew Bonar Law*, Eyre and Spottiswoode, 1955
Frank Owen, *Tempestuous Journey: Lloyd George, His Life and Times*,
    Hutchinson, 1954
John Grigg, *Lloyd George*, vol. I, *The Young Lloyd George*; vol. II, *The
    People's Champion*; vol. III, *From Peace to War, 1912–16*, Methuen,
    1973, 1978 and 1985
John Campbell, *Lloyd George: the Goat in the Wilderness, 1922–31*,
    Jonathan Cape, 1977
David Marquand, *Ramsay MacDonald*, Jonathan Cape, 1977
Stephen McKenna, *Reginald McKenna*, Eyre and Spottiswoode, 1948
Harold Nicolson, *Diaries and Letters, 1930–9*, Collins, 1966
Charles Stuart (ed.), *The Reith Diaries*, Collins, 1975
Viscount Samuel, *Memoirs*, Cresset Press, 1945
Gregory Blaxland, *J. H. Thomas. A Life for Unity*, Muller, 1964
Lord Vansittart, *The Mist Procession*, Hutchinson, 1958
Norman and Jeanne Mackenzie (eds.), *The Diary of Beatrice Webb*,
    vol. III, *1905–24* and vol. IV, *1924–43*, Virago, 1984 and 1985

A. J. P. Taylor, *English History, 1914–1945*, Oxford University Press,
    1965
R. Page Arnot, *The Miners: Years of Struggle*, Allen and Unwin, 1953

Index

Compiled by Douglas Matthews

Labour Party: rise to power, 14–16; SB
encourages, 15, 70, 72; and Law
government, 55; SB predicts
government by, 58, 71; 1923 election
success, 77–8; 1923 minority
government, 78, 82; 1924 election
results, 83; and Communist Party, 83;
1929 election success, 107–8; 1929
government, 109–10, 122–3, 126;
1930 conference, 122; and National
Government, 123–4, 129, 132–3;
1931 election losses, 131; in 1930s by-
elections, 134; and rearmament, 160
Lang, Cosmo Gordon, Archbishop of
Canterbury, 140; biography, 179
Laski, Harold, 138
Lausanne, Conference of (1922–3), 49n
Laval, Pierre, 139, 142, 173
Law, Andrew Bonar: ministers, 35; and
SB's attitude to money, 37; age, 39;
political ambitions, 40; as Chancellor,
41–2; resigns (1921), 46–7, 136; on
Chanak crisis, 49n; ill-health, 51–2,
57, 59; seen as alternative to Lloyd
George, 51–2; as Prime Minister, 54,
57, 69, 131; and war debts, 56–7;
1923 resignation and succession,
59–60, 62; speed of work, 64; and
Beaverbrook, 167; appoints
Boscawen, 168; and Jones, 174;
dislikes Waterhouse, 180
League of Nations Union, 136, 169
Lever, Sir Hardman, 41
Liberal Party: dissensions, 15; and Law's
government, 55; declines, 70, 72;
1923 election gains, 77; 1924 election
losses, 83; 1929 election losses,
107–8; and MacDonald Labour
government, 122–3; and National
Government, 126, 129, 132; and
rearmament, 160
Literary Fund, 99
Lloyd George, David, 1st Earl: SB's
attitude to, 15, 43–4, 46–7, 67, 70–2,
109; classlessness, 16; and social
inequality, 22; experience, 26;
leadership, 27, 160; political
ambitions, 40; in First World War, 41;
1921 coalition government, 46, 51,
54, 100; and honours system, 47–8;
and Chanak crisis, 49; SB attacks
leadership, 50–4; resigns, 54–5, 69;
SB replies to in Commons, 58;

interferes with Departments, 65;
reading, 66; cynicism, 68; Curzon on,
70n; and trade protection, 71, 73, 77;
in SB's *People* interview, 82; and
unions' Triple Alliance, 95n;
journalism, 109; dynamism, 131; on
Derby, 171; and Jones, 174
Locarno, Treaty of, 89–90
London Economic Conference, 1933, 20
Londonderry, Charles Stewart Henry
Vane-Tempest-Stewart, 7th Marquess
of, 138n
Londonderry, Edith, Marchioness of (née
Chaplin), 132
Lothian, Philip Kerr, 11th Marquess of,
144n
Low, Sir David, 140; biography, 180
Lyons, Joseph Aloysius, 152

MacDonald, James Ramsay: weak
governments, 15; as leader, 16; and
General Strike, 17; and economics, 20;
and social inequality, 23; and defence,
23; SB's mild opposition to, 30; SB
replies to in Commons, 58; working
methods, 68; and 1923 election, 77;
forms minority government (1923),
78–9, 82; and Jones, 81; and Zinoviev
letter, 82n; broadcasts, 83; in 1929
election, 107; Labour government,
110, 122; and unemployment, 122;
heads National Government, 124,
126, 128, 131–4; and 1931 financial
crisis, 125–6; decline, 131–2, 135;
resignation, 135; and Abdication, 158;
SB's tribute to, 162
Macleod, Iain, 13; *Neville Chamberlain*,
24
Macmillan, Lady Dorothy (née
Cavendish), 172
Macmillan, Harold, 1st Earl of Stockton,
21, 86, 172
Margesson, David, 1st Viscount, 143;
biography, 180
Masterman, C. F. G., 168
Maurice, Major-General Sir Frederick,
43–4; biography, 175
May, Sir George, 122, 125
McKenna, Reginald, 54–5, 57, 69, 168;
biography, 180
Middlemas, Keith and Barnes, John:
Baldwin, 12, 126n
Milner, Alfred, Viscount, 144n

Miners' Federation, 106
Monckton, Sir Walter, 1st Viscount,
153–4; biography, 181
Mond-Turner talks, 19, 106
Moore-Brabazon, Col. J. T. C. *see*
Brabazon, 1st Baron
Morgan, J. P., and Company, New York,
129
Mosley, Diana, Lady (*née* Mitford),
176
Mosley, Sir Oswald, 122, 178;
biography, 182
Munich agreement, 1938, 24–5, 164
Mussolini, Benito, 14, 139, 178, 180

National Government: Bevin and, 18;
and unemployment, 21; proposed,
126–8; formed, 129; composition and
operations, 132–5
News Chronicle, 153
Nicolson, Sir Harold, 157;
biography, 182 *Arketall*, 49*n*;
Noel-Baker, Philip, Baron, 170
Norfolk, Bernard Marmaduke FitzAlan-
Howard, 16th Duke of, 148
Norman, Montagu, Baron Norman of St
Clere, 56, 90, 125, 161*n*; biography,
183
Novar, Ronald Munro-Ferguson,
Viscount, 57, 74; biography, 183

Ottawa Conference *see* Imperial
Preference Conference

Paddington South by-election (1929),
116–18
Palmerston, Henry John Temple, 3rd
Viscount, 35*n*
Peace Ballot, 136
Peace Society, 27, 138
Peel, Sir Robert, 35*n*
People (newspaper), 81–2
Petter, Sir Ernest, 118
Plymouth *see* Conservative Party:
Conferences
Poincaré, Raymond, 68
Poynter, Edward, 32
Pretyman, Ernest, 54*n*
prices, 22
protection (trade), 19, 71–6, 130
Pugh, Sir Arthur, 99–100; biography,
183
Pym, Francis, 13

Queen Mary (ship), 22
Queen's Hall: SB's 1931 speech, 119

Raymond, John (ed.): *The Baldwin Age*,
12
Reagan, Ronald, 28
rearmament, 21–2, 158–9
Reith, Sir John, 1st Baron, 102, 145;
biography, 184
Rhineland, 25
Richards, Thomas, 178
Robinson, Sir Joseph, 48
Roosevelt, Franklin D., 27, 158
Roosevelt, Theodore, 96 & *n*
Rose, Kenneth: *George V*, 61*n*, 145*n*,
179
Rosebery, Archibald Philip Primrose, 5th
Earl of, 59
Rothermere, Harold Sidney
Harmsworth, 1st Baron, 110–11,
114–15, 117, 120, 147; biography,
184
Royal Empire Society, 117
Royal Society of St George, 31

'Safety first' slogan and policy, 20, 107,
111
Salisbury, James Edward Hubert
Gascoyne-Cecil, 4th Marquess of:
supports SB, 51; and SB's succession
as Prime Minister, 59–60, 160–1;
favours free trade, 74; in SB Cabinet,
89; and Abdication crisis, 148; on
rearmament, 159; biography, 178
Salisbury, Robert Arthur Talbot
Gascoyne-Cecil, 3rd Marquess of, 59,
85
Salvidge, Sir Archibald, 79
Samuel, Sir Herbert, 1st Viscount, 18,
25, 96–7, 104, 128, 130, 132;
biography, 185
Sankey, John, Viscount, 130, 133;
biography, 185.
Savage, Michael Joseph, 152
Seven Hours Act, 1919, 104
Sèvres, Treaty of (1920), 48*n*
Simpson, Edward, 146–7
Simpson, Mrs Wallis (*later* Duchess of
Windsor), 146–7, 149–51, 154–6,
158, 163
Smith, Herbert, 17, 98, 177; biography,
186
Smyrna, 48*n*